MOSAIC
GARDEN
PROJECTS

Mosaic Garden Projects

Add Color to Your Garden with Tables, Fountains, Birdbaths, and More

by Mark Brody

with Sheila Ashdown

with photographs by Justin Myers

Timber Press
Portland / London

page 1: A shimmering dragonfly combines several kinds of glass to stunning effect.
pages 2–3: A mosaicked pagoda offers a bright and modern take on the traditional pagoda form.

The information in this book is true and complete to the best of our knowledge. All recommendations are made without guarantee on the part of the author or Timber Press. The author and publisher disclaim any liability in connection with the use of this information. Mention of trademark, proprietary product, or vendor does not constitute a guarantee or warranty of the product by the publisher or authors and does not imply its approval to the exclusion of other products or vendors.

Published in 2015 by Timber Press, Inc.

Photo credits appear on page 298.
Illustrations pages 174, 196, and 246 by Kate Francis
Illustration page 63 by Sarah Loveday, courtesy of Andy Vernon
Templates by Mark Brody

The Haseltine Building
133 S.W. Second Avenue, Suite 450
Portland, Oregon 97204-3527
timberpress.com

6a Lonsdale Road
London NW6 6RD
timberpress.co.uk

Printed in China
Book design by Breanna Goodrow

Library of Congress Cataloging-in-Publication Data
Brody, Mark, author.
  Mosaic garden projects: add color to your garden with tables, fountains, birdbaths, and more/by Mark Brody; with Sheila Ashdown; with photographs by Justin Myers.
     pages cm
  Includes index.
  ISBN 978-1-60469-487-1
  1. Gardens—Design. 2. Mosaics. 3. Color in design. 4. Garden ornaments and furniture. I. Ashdown, Sheila. II. Title.
  SB473.B7226 2015
  712—dc23

                          2014020734

A catalog record for this book is also available from the British Library.

To my lovely wife, Jo,
who can always put the pieces together
quicker than I can.
I'm just so grateful to be near
your infectious charm and spontaneity.

To my mother, Peggy,
whose artistic side has fully blossomed
and who has always been the biggest fan
of my creativity.

—M. B.

Contents

MOSAIC FUNDAMENTALS

MOSAIC PROJECTS 71

PROJECT TEMPLATES 267

Preface

My interest in mosaics grew out of my adventure with building a house. My wife, Jo, and I built our starter house out of tires, tin cans, and adobe brick in the high desert of New Mexico. We built an Earthship—a house made out of recycled materials—and learned which surfaces could stand up to the ever-changing elements of the seasons. We tiled our adobe walls (a failure), bathroom showers (very inspiring), and kitchen countertops (very practical), and soon mosaics spread to our home's outdoor features as well. Tiles provided an ornamental and protective surface to the form underneath and, in our garden, became a colorful accent that could outlast any coat of paint.

A wealth of materials and surfaces can be covered with mosaic, and knowing the possibilities of mosaic as well as the limitations is vital to confidently making an art piece for the outdoors. I taught myself how to mosaic, learning techniques from one project to the next, and I relish the puzzle-like quality of mosaics—putting many pieces together to make a whole. I've been teaching mosaic for more than 12 years, and in each student I see an innate fascination with putting together shapes and color in a unique way. In this book, I provide an introduction to the tools, materials, designs, and basic methods or techniques for a variety of projects that will get you started. While there are specific techniques to laying out a mosaic, there is also room for innovation. After completing your first two or three mosaic projects, you will likely develop a style of your own.

Mosaic and garden design have similar characteristics. They are each made of an assembly of pieces laid out in a certain way. You can give 20 gardeners the same list of plants, and they will each design a garden in their own style. So, find a mosaic you would like to make and don't worry if you change a color here or a size there—this book is just planting the seeds for your next garden creation.

This ambitious
project is well
worth the
effort. Your
senses will
delight in the
whimsical
design and
flowing
cascade of
water.

Plant Some Art in Your Garden

osaics provide a creative finishing touch to any garden. No matter the season, mosaic adds an element of delight year-round. When your garden is in bloom, the mosaic recedes, letting Mother Nature have her time to shine. And in the winter months, mosaics emerge to give some much-needed life to a dormant landscape.

What sets mosaic apart from most other art forms is its functionality and endurance. Though mosaics are pleasing to the eye, they can be so much more. Even ordinary objects can become extraordinary. The projects in this book feature planters, tables, a birdbath, fountains, and more. Of course, a mosaic doesn't need to have an explicit purpose. After all, does a flower need a reason to exist? Not at all. Its beauty is reason enough.

What's more, these lovely art pieces are built to last for years outdoors with hardly any upkeep. In fact, there still exist preserved mosaics that were created in 3000 BCE.

Talk about a perennial! Because they are made from building materials—especially those borrowed from the tiling trade—mosaic has just the right blend of beauty and strength to make it an art form that can go from indoors to outdoors. Composing a mosaic from hundreds of small pieces is a painstaking process, but it's a worthwhile investment to create something that will possibly last a lifetime. This durability gives you the freedom to push the boundaries of art and how you can enjoy it. Rather than being hidden away indoors, your garden mosaic can live outside and become part of the landscape.

Mosaic art has deep roots in history—all the way back to the fourth century BCE. Mosaic was born because, given the tools available at the time, craftsmen had to work with smaller materials to lay floors. Some cultures began to add an artistic element to something that was otherwise just purely functional. And then they added it to the walls! As tools evolved, the emphasis grew toward the artistry and craft. Mosaic became less necessary, but more beautiful. If you're a gardener, you can likely appreciate the opportunity to participate in an art form that has been cultivated and tended across centuries.

If you're new to mosaic, rest assured that, if you're a gardener, you're already bringing a necessary set of skills to the

> **Outside is where art should live, amongst us.**
> —BANKSY

process. Mosaic has many similarities to garden design, because each uses similar components. The composition of a garden, as well as any mosaic, is a product of its colors, shapes, sizes, and layout of materials. Experience teaches the gardener to look at the big picture and know which plants work well placed next to another plant. Similarly, the mosaic artist knows when to keep color tones the same and when to punch out a strong contrast. Every new piece laid out, whether it's a plant in the garden or a tile in the mosaic, is part of the larger design.

The challenge of making mosaics for the garden is to learn the proper materials and techniques to make something creative and enduring. This book is loaded with 25 exciting mosaic projects with step-by-step directions, photographs, and templates, as well as comprehensive information about materials and techniques to help you create beautiful, long-lasting artwork for your garden.

Mosaic can transform an ordinary planter into a work of art.

11

MOSAIC
FUNDAMENTALS

Here I am in my studio, surrounded by the tools of the trade. To make the strawberry mosaic, follow the directions for the Avocado mosaic on page 105.

Caddies keep sheets of stained glass safe, organized, and visible, and plastic bins are ideal for organizing smaller pieces of glass.

▼

Work Space

 efore you begin to create mosaic art, it's important to have a comfortable work space and some basic tools, supplies, and safety equipment. Mosaic artists can create beautiful work in humble surroundings, so there are few work space considerations beyond those required for comfort and safety.

- **TABLE AND CHAIR** Mosaics take hours to complete, usually over the course of days. So you'll need a worktable that is not only large and sturdy enough to accommodate the weight and dimensions of your piece, but is also in an out-of-the-way place. In other words, don't mosaic at your dinner table. You can sit or stand while you work; whichever feels most comfortable to you. However, if you prefer to stand, use a rubber floor mat for comfort.
- **STORAGE** The more you mosaic, the more tools, supplies, and materials you'll collect. Stay organized with ample bins, boxes, and caddies for storage. Don't plan on using your worktable for storage, because it will become crowded quickly. Separate shelves or a secondary table are best. Caddies are excellent for storing large sheets of glass, while bins are good for smaller pieces.
- **LIGHT AND VENTILATION** Mosaic is detailed work, so make sure your work space is well lit. And good ventilation is crucial when you're working with dusty grouts and smelly sealants.
- **ACCESS TO WATER** You'll use water for mixing adhesive and grout, as well as for cleaning up, so your work space should have easy access to a water supply.

Tools and Supplies

All the tools and supplies you need for making mosaics are easily available online or at hardware and craft-supply stores. Because mosaic is rooted in the industrial arts, the tools and materials listed here—along with the materials of the mosaics themselves—are commercially available wherever you can find home-building supplies. Some specialized suppliers are also listed in Resources.

Basic Mosaic Tools and Supplies

PISTOL-GRIP OR STANDARD GLASS CUTTER for scoring straight and gently curved lines on the surface of glass

GLASS RUNNER for snapping glass along a scored line

TWO-WHEELED NIPPERS for creating short curves and as a trimming tool for glass

CERAMIC TILE NIPPERS for cutting ceramic

CIRCLE CUTTER for cutting circular shapes (optional)

CUTTING BOARD to catch and contain small shards of glass and keep your work surface clean (I like the cutting boards made by Morton Systems.)

SANDING BLOCK to take away sharp edges

FIBERGLASS MESH TAPE (2 in. wide) for preparing the edges of the substrate

STICKY MESH to use as a temporary working surface for your mosaic. My favorite is 36-inch FibaTape wall-repair fabric, which is a lightweight fiberglass mesh.

ROCK TUMBLER (optional) for taking the sharp edges off tesserae

TWEEZERS for handling small tesserae

CLEAR CONTACT PAPER to secure tesserae when setting your composition in adhesive

VELLUM PAPER for transferring designs

FELT-TIP MARKERS for marking score lines on glass

PENCILS for sketching

ERASERS

Tools for working with glass tesserae
(displayed on the cutting board on the left side):

1. Streaked stained glass
2. Stained glass
3. Tweezers (for seating small tesserae)
4. Pistol-grip glass cutter
5. Two-wheeled nipper
6. Sanding block (this one is metal)
7. Glass runner (also called a splitter)
8. Standard glass cutter

The cutting board underneath the tools is designed to catch and hold shards of glass.

Tools for working with ceramic tesserae
(displayed on the right):

9. Ceramic tile samples
10. Ceramic tile samples
11. Ceramic tile nipper
12. X-Acto knife (for cutting wedi board)
13. Carpenter's square (for measuring and cutting substrates)

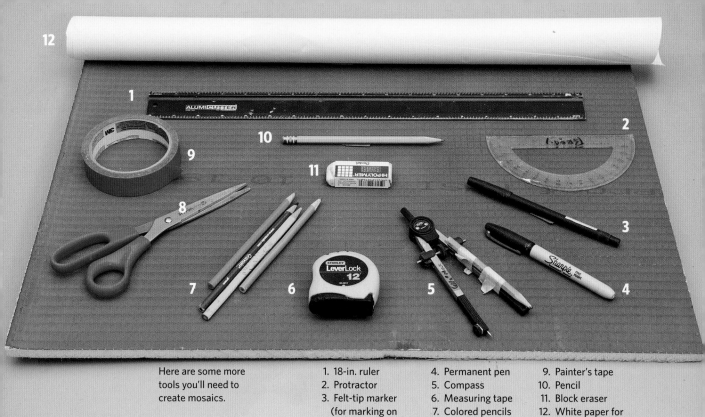

Here are some more tools you'll need to create mosaics.

1. 18-in. ruler
2. Protractor
3. Felt-tip marker (for marking on glass)
4. Permanent pen
5. Compass
6. Measuring tape
7. Colored pencils
8. Scissors
9. Painter's tape
10. Pencil
11. Block eraser
12. White paper for sketching cartoons

PAINTER'S TAPE OR MASKING TAPE to affix a cartoon to the substrate

SCISSORS

COMPASS AND PROTRACTOR for creating circular pieces

METAL RULER for measuring and for cutting a straight line of glass

DIGITAL CAMERA for documenting work and a day's progress (It's so important!)

NEEDLE-NOSE PLIERS for cutting wires for hanging mosaics

HANGERS AND SCREWS for hanging mosaics

CORDLESS SCREWDRIVER for hanging mosaics

WET SAW for cutting custom ceramic pieces

SMALL BUCKETS to hold grout, water, or glass shards

WOOD BOARD for turning mosaics over or sliding mosaics into place

Adhesive and Grouting Materials and Tools

- Thin-set mortar, dry or premixed (for most mosaic projects)
- Silicone adhesive (for glass-on-glass or glass-on-acrylic-plastic projects)

SAFETY CONSIDERATIONS

While mosaic is generally a safe endeavor, I recommend taking basic safety precautions to protect yourself against the inevitable sharp edges, glass shards, and dust that are created during the process. If you have small children or pets, be sure to keep them away from your work space. Before you begin, invest in:

- Safety glasses to wear while cutting tesserae
- A dust mask to wear when mixing adhesives and grout
- Latex gloves to wear while mixing adhesives and grout
- A dust pan and brush to clean tables and floors
- Bandages and a first-aid kit for patching up minor wounds
- An apron to keep shards of glass and stains off your clothes

Some of the essential supplies you'll need for safety and cleaning up include an apron, dust pan and brush, mask, safety glasses, and gloves.

Also, just as a day in the garden can cause aches and pains, so can hours spent immersed in mosaic. Be sure to guard against sore muscles by creating an ergonomic work space and taking breaks to stretch your back, arms, and shoulders.

- Notched trowel for spreading thin-set mortar
- Small trowel for applying thin-set mortar to small areas
- Sandwich bags for making piping bags
- Flat mixing trowel
- Small buckets for mixing
- Matte board for applying silicone glue to glass
- Cementitious grout (for most mosaic projects)
- Urethane grout (for heavy-use projects, especially for mosaics that will be in contact with water)
- Rubber trowel (also called a float) for spreading grout
- Cotton cloths for polishing the finished mosaic
- Small sponges for shaping grouted shoulders

Materials: Tesserae, Substrates, Adhesives, and Grouts

osaic is a flexible medium that encourages the creative use of materials. However, when creating mosaic art for your garden, it's important to choose materials that will withstand the weather. If you live in a climate with considerable cold temperatures and precipitation, then your mosaics will likely be subject to freeze-thaw cycles that can erode some of the less-hardy materials. In this case, you should choose the more durable options recommended in this book. Mosaic art is an investment of time and money—it would be a shame to see that investment go to pieces in rough weather. Another option, of course, is to bring your mosaic inside for the winter—this is especially crucial for mosaics with horizontal surfaces, such as tabletops, which are prone to collecting water.

Weather considerations aside, rest assured that most of the projects in this book feature tesserae, substrates, grouts, and adhesives that will retain their strength and beauty for years to come, through rain or shine.

Tesserae

Tesserae (tessera in the singular) are the many small pieces that you put together to form a mosaic. Almost any durable material can be transformed into a tessera, as long as you can seal it and glue it. Following are the types you'll encounter in this book.

Tesserae are the many small pieces that compose a mosaic.

STAINED GLASS

Stained-glass tesserae are an excellent choice for mosaics destined for the garden. They're durable and weather-resistant, and they're available in a wide variety of textures and colors. You can find stained glass that is rippled, smooth, iridescent, opaque, translucent, or swirled, providing endless opportunities for mixing and matching. One advantage to working with stained glass is that it is sold by the sheet, which allows you to cut custom shapes, big or small. You can also cut a large sheet of stained glass into a bank, or supply, of unusually shaped tesserae.

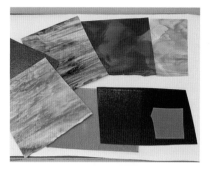

Sheets of stained glass, which are available in a range of colors and textures.

VITREOUS GLASS

Vitreous-glass tesserae are durable and beautiful. The ridged underside of vitreous glass grips well to adhesive, creating a strong bond with the substrate of a mosaic. And, vitreous glass is waterproof, which makes it especially well-suited for use in mosaics that will be in frequent or constant contact with water, such as a fountain or birdbath. Vitreous glass comes in square tiles of relatively uniform size, typically ⅜ or ¾ of an inch. You can buy vitreous glass in sheets by the square foot or as precut tiles by the pound. Precut tiles are excellent for creating a uniform or tidy effect, especially in the background or border of a mosaic.

An array of vitreous-glass tesserae. Long-lasting and waterproof, vitreous glass is ideal for outdoor mosaics.

MILLEFIORI

These distinctive round tesserae are the product of a specialized glass-making technique that involves layering multiple colors into a cane of glass; when the cane is cut on the cross-section, an interior pattern is revealed: flowers, stars, concentric circles, and more. These eye-catching tesserae are excellent for adding variety to your mosaic design. You can buy millefiori cane and cut it yourself, but it's more commonly sold in packages of precut millefiori pieces instead.

Millefiori slices can add personality to a mosaic.

Here are some examples of ceramic tiles. They have a rougher surface than glass does, and it's more difficult to make a straight cut on ceramic (unless you use a wet saw), but their rough-cut quality gives a mosaic a distinctive look.

Outdoor mosaics with mirrored tesserae sparkle when sunlight catches them.

CERAMIC

Ceramic is a popular choice for mosaic artists because it's inexpensive, widely available, and comes in a variety of colors, patterns, and glazes. You can find ceramic tiles in various shapes and sizes. Four-inch-square tiles are the most common, but you can also find smaller squares (one inch or three-quarter inch), along with rectangles and thin rectangles.

When selecting ceramic, it's important to consider the effect of glazing. Unglazed ceramic holds up the best in severe weather conditions. It's available in a range of earth tones, and its flat, matte appearance will blend harmoniously with a garden. Glazed ceramic, on the other hand, is available in an array of eye-popping colors, but it's not ideal for outdoor use, because the glaze can fade and crack with repeated weathering over the years. If you're keen on using glazed ceramic, be sure to choose tiles that are rated for outdoor use. A good rule of thumb to know is that the shinier or more crackled the glaze, the less durable the ceramic. That said, new high-fire glazes have been developed that hold up well outdoors. And if your climate is mild, your mosaic will likely endure for years. If you're concerned about weathering, plan on keeping your mosaic out of the elements during winter.

MIRROR

Mirrored tesserae are a fun addition to a mosaic, making it wink in the sunlight on a bright day. Just make sure that you attach any mirrored tesserae with silicone glue or mirror adhesive—other adhesives, such as thin-set mortar, will corrode the mirror's reflective backing.

SMALTI TILE

Smalti tile is an opaque glass that is handcrafted in Italy and Mexico and has been used in mosaic for centuries. It is sometimes referred to as Byzantine-glass mosaic tile, because during the Byzantine era smalti was highly regarded in places like the Hagia Sophia in Constantinople. Though smalti is more expensive than other types of tesserae, it has a distinctive texture and is available in an amazing variety of colors.

It's often adhered with its riven—or cut—side up, to best showcase its rough-hewn nature and characteristic air bubbles.

FUSED GLASS

Fused glass is made by layering and heating glass until it melts, or fuses, together. Fused-glass pieces contribute interesting focal points to a mosaic. Many cities have fused-glass studios, where you can either purchase ready-made fused glass, place custom orders, or make your own designs.

PEBBLES

It won't surprise you to hear that pebbles make excellent tesserae for outdoor mosaics. They can present a technical challenge if their sizes vary greatly, but their muted earth tones will feel right at home in a garden. You can purchase pebbles in bulk—smooth river rock is especially nice—or simply use pebbles you've collected.

FOUND OBJECTS

Found objects supply a unique addition to a mosaic. They add visual interest and texture, and are a fun way to reuse items that have otherwise outlived their function—like the worn-out tools I use in the Fix It mosaic on page 182. Found objects can be almost anything: broken pottery, beaded jewelry, flat-back marbles, plumbing parts, various bits of stone or metal, and more. As long as the object has a flat surface for adhesive, it can have a place of honor in your mosaic. Using found objects adds to the time it takes to complete a project, because each object needs to be set individually, but they're worth the effort.

Making fused glass is an art form in itself. I used the ladybug at left in the Hosta Leaf mosaic, the flower in the Neighborhood Library mosaic, and the leaf at right in the Pouring Pitchers mosaic.

Here are a few colorful examples of smalti.

Pebbles can be purchased at craft and art-supply stores.

Flat-back marbles can be used as eyes in animal mosaics or to provide additional flair to a mosaic.

CUTTING AND SHAPING TESSERAE

When you're cutting and shaping tesserae for a mosaic, try to embrace variety and not get too hung up on uniformity. The little differences and irregularities in tesserae are what make mosaic such a homey, cozy addition to your garden.

Safety Note
When you're cutting glass and ceramic, always wear safety glasses to protect your eyes from stray shards.

Cutting Glass Tesserae

Cutting glass is an essential skill for a mosaic artist, and a few basic tools and some practice will take you far. Usually, a design calls for a bank, or supply, of basic shapes—such as squares, triangles, and trapezoids—plus a number of customized pieces cut to a near-exact shape and size. The techniques shown here will help you cut a range of glass tesserae. Most first-timers are astonished by how easy these techniques are. When I cut glass for the first time, I instantly knew that this was a material that would allow for much more control and customization than the ceramic tile I'd been using previously.

Materials
- Small container for discarded shards
- Vellum paper (optional)
- Pencil (optional)
- Safety glasses
- Rock tumbler (optional)

Tools
- Sheet of stained glass or vitreous glass tiles
- Pistol-grip glass cutter
- Glass runner
- Two-wheeled nipper
- Cutting board
- Sanding block
- Felt-tip marker

Basic Glass-Cutting Technique

1. **Score the glass.** To score lines that are straight or gently curved, you'll use a pistol-grip glass cutter. Place a sheet of glass, smooth side up, on your cutting board. Place the tip of the glass cutter on the surface of the glass, 1/4 in. away from the bottom edge (cutting from bottom to top allows you to see where you're going). Raise your wrist to set the cutting wheel on the glass, and then cut the score firmly, applying even pressure from start to finish. The sound of the wheel scratching the surface of the glass is a familiar one in mosaic studios. If you score too lightly, the glass won't break cleanly. And once the glass is scored, it's inadvisable to score it again.

2. **Run the score.** Once you've scored a straight line (or gently curved line, if that's the shape you need), you'll break—or run—the glass with a glass runner. The head of the glass runner has a small line running perpendicular to its edge; the tool is designed to exert an even amount of pressure on both sides of this line. Simply match the line on the head of the glass runner with the line of the score on the glass. Then squeeze the runner firmly and quickly to break the score cleanly.

Use a glass runner to break the score when you're cutting glass.

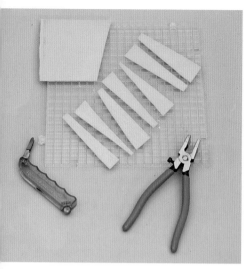

I used a glass runner and a pistol-grip glass cutter to cut these long, tapered triangles.

Cutting Straight-Edged Shapes

Using a pistol-grip glass cutter and a glass runner, you can easily create a variety of straight-edged shapes such as squares, trapezoids, and triangles. Use a metal ruler or do this freehand—a mosaic does not need perfect measurements and cuts.

Safety Note
If a tessera has an especially sharp edge, dull it with a sanding block to avoid cutting yourself.

Long, red stick-shaped tesserae.

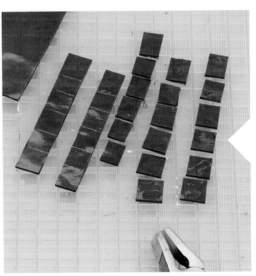

Here are some examples of paper stencils and tesserae in the shape of trapezoids and parallelograms.

These small squares are for my bank of tesserae. I broke the squares along the scored lines.

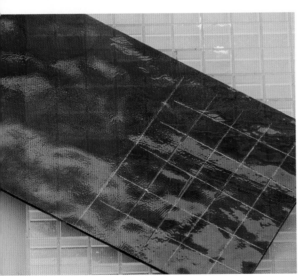

Cutting Gently Curved Shapes

While you can't achieve circles with a pistol-grip glass cutter, you can create gentle curves. Scoring the glass is done similarly as described above, but you create a curved score by moving your entire arm in a curved motion. When running the score, position the glass runner so that the head is as close to the center of the scored line as possible. This will help ensure a clean cut.

Use a pistol-grip glass cutter to cut gentle curves to create leaf-shaped tesserae.

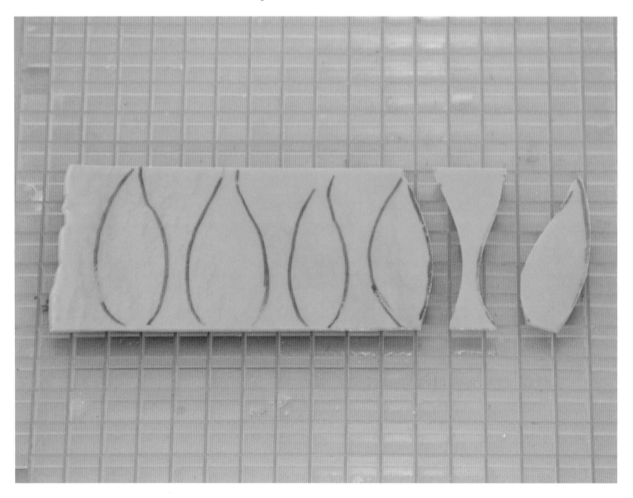

Cutting Circles

Cutting a perfect circle of glass is possible when you use a circle cutter. There are two types of circle cutters: one will create circles that are one to five inches in diameter, and the other will cut circles from four to twenty-four inches in diameter. Learning to use a circle cutter is a bit challenging, and the wheel on the circle cutter needs to be replaced every 25 to 50 circles, but it's worth the effort if you want beautiful circles. If you prefer not to cut your own circles, you can order precut circles from some tile manufacturers.

This is a circle cutter, which you can use if you want to cut perfect circles yourself instead of buying them.

To estimate how much glass you'll need to complete your mosaic, lay a piece of glass over the area to be filled, and then consider the fact that the glass will be split and the interstices grouted—in effect, the glass sheet could grow by about 25 percent. With that in mind, estimate how far the piece will go.

Using a Two-Wheeled Nipper for Unique Shapes

The two-wheeled nipper is a versatile tool that allows you to cut curves and to nibble the tesserae into the shapes you desire. Unlike the glass-cutting methods considered so far, which require two tools—a glass cutter and glass runner—a two-wheeled nipper is a one-stop tool that cuts glass directly. Hold the nipper with the wheels facing you, and place the glass in the nipper's wheels; the glass will break at the point where the wheeled blades meet the surface. This method requires a bit of force, so have a container on hand to catch any glass pieces that might fly off. Angle the nipper so that the glass is directed into the container, and break the glass by squeezing the nipper handles with firm pressure. You can modify a tessera—and even create a rough circle—by nibbling its edges with the nipper. You can also use the nipper to create irregular, whisker-like tesserae.

Using Vellum Paper for Custom Shapes

There are times when you'll want to cut stained glass into a tessera of a particular shape and size. This can be done easily with transparent vellum paper. Simply lay a piece of vellum over the cartoon (the drawing that serves as the basis of your mosaic design; we'll discuss them later in Mosaic Design Basics). The lines of the cartoon should be visible through the thin vellum (if they're not, remove the vellum and use a felt-tip marker to darken the lines). Use a pencil to trace the desired shape on the vellum, and then cut out the shape. This is the stencil you will use to draw the design on the stained glass. Place the stencil on the stained glass sheet and trace around it with a felt-tip marker. Then score the glass along the outline and cut the glass as usual. After cutting the glass, use a cotton cloth to wipe off any marks left by the vellum.

Maybe you'll want to add a small piece of a similar colored glass to lend some variety to your bank of tesserae. Estimating how much glass you'll need is an inexact science, but if you cut too much, you can always keep it on hand for a future mosaic.

Making a Bank of Glass

When you're cutting a sheet of stained glass, it's most economical to cut large, custom shapes first and then use the rest of the glass, as needed, to cut a bank of tesserae in various shapes and sizes. Cutting large or custom shapes inevitably creates odds-and-ends pieces, and you can usually minimize waste by incorporating them into your bank. In general, having a bank of tesserae speeds up the mosaic process. For instance, if you plan on creating a mosaic with blue sky as the background, you can cut a bank of blue glass to have at the ready. How do you know what shape to use in your bank? Or which shapes will work best for the area you need to fill? These are questions you'll be able to answer as you gain more experience creating mosaics. The sections on *opera* and *andamento* explain different possibilities for shaping and laying tesserae.

Tumbling Tesserae

Though you can use a sanding block to smooth the sharp edges of glass tesserae, a rock tumbler will save you a lot of effort—especially when you need to tumble an entire mosaic's worth of tesserae. With three-

To stay organized while you work, separate colored tiles using plates or bowls.

dimensional pieces, such as the Jeweled Frog Planter, there's a greater chance that a sharp edge will protrude from the grout. To prevent that, tumble the glass tiles before you begin to seat them. I use a child's rock tumbler—nothing fancy—that tumbles about a square foot of glass at a time. This is also a good habit to get into if you work on mosaics with kids. If you tumble the glass tesserae before you start working, their little hands will be protected from nicks and cuts. If you're working on a two-dimensional mosaic, you won't need tumbled glass tesserae.

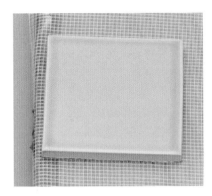

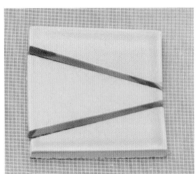

Starting with a square ceramic tile, I cut these tapered tesserae with a wet saw.

Cutting Ceramic Tesserae

When you're working with ceramic tesserae, you have to be comfortable with the luck of the draw. It's impossible to get a precise, straight cut on ceramic without using a wet saw, which might seem overly work-intensive to the casual mosaic artist. However, often the rough-cut quality of ceramic is exactly what makes it appealing, as it lends a raw and immediate look to a mosaic.

Materials	Tools
• Ceramic tiles	• Ceramic tile nipper
	• Wet saw
	• Hammer
	• Small container for discarded shards
	• Safety glasses

Basic Ceramic-Cutting Techniques

There are three options for cutting ceramic: a wet saw, a tile nipper, and a hammer. If your design calls for straight-edged tesserae, then a wet saw is the best tool. It carries a greater degree of difficulty, but if you're up for the challenge, a wet saw allows you to achieve crisp edges and clean lines that are otherwise unattainable with ceramic. With a wet saw, you can cut a tile in half or in sticks, and you can cut tapered shapes.

A tile nipper is the second option. There's not much technique to using the nipper—it's mostly brute force. Simply take your tile (or your ceramic plate, if that's what you're using) and place the mouth of the nipper where you'd like to break the tile. Then, holding the tile over a container (to catch any pieces that might fly off), squeeze the nipper handles firmly until the ceramic breaks.

The third option is a hammer. Using a hammer to break ceramic offers the least amount of control, but it's a quick way to create a bank of irregularly shaped tesserae. To break a ceramic tile or plate, place the tile in a piece of thick cloth (such as a bath towel) and lay it on the floor.

Plywood, cement backer board, clear glass, medium density fiberboard, wedi board, and (in the back) a precast cement form.

A well-aimed hit with the hammer is all it takes to break the tile into three to four pieces. Then you can use a nipper to cut custom shapes out of the pieces, if you like.

For the most diverse set of tesserae, mix all three options—a wet saw, a tile nipper, and a hammer. For example, if you cut a batch of ceramic sticks using a wet saw, you can then use a tile nipper to break the sticks into charmingly irregular shapes.

Substrates

A substrate is the foundation of a mosaic. Given the flexible nature of mosaic, you can use almost anything as a substrate, but there are a few that are better for the outdoors. Since the mosaics in this book were designed to live in gardens, I chose substrates for their durability and weather-resistance, as well as their ease of use. When you're choosing a substrate for a mosaic you'd like to hang, consider how heavy the finished piece will be and what kind of hanging device will be the best for mounting it.

Safety Note

When you're cleaning your worktable, use a brush—not your hands—to sweep the surface clear of shards. It's helpful to keep a container (such as an empty yogurt container or paint can) on hand to hold shards and other discarded bits. When the container is full, put a lid on it and dispose of it in a garbage can.

Be sure to install your hanging mechanism before you create the mosaic. That way, you won't inadvertently damage the piece of art after it's finished.

WEDI BOARD

Wedi board (pronounced "weedy") is an expanded polystyrene foam core overlaid on both sides with a cement coating. It's a construction material typically used for tiling bathroom showers, so it's designed to be long-lasting and resistant to moisture—perfect for all seasons in your garden. It works well for mosaics because it's lightweight, doesn't require a sealant, and—best of all—you can use a utility knife to easily cut it into whatever shape suits your design. However, though wedi is highly versatile, the manufacturer does not recommend using it for horizontal installations such as tabletops—it may not be strong enough to support both the mosaic and items set on the table.

GUIDE TO SUBSTRATES

	Adhesive	Hanger	Preparation before Mosaic
wedi	thin-set mortar or AcrylPro	D-screws and wire on plywood adhered to wedi	tape and apply thin-set mortar to the edges
MDF wood	AcrylPro	D-screws and wire	seal wood with 50:50 glue:water
plywood	thin-set mortar	D-screws and wire or French cleat	wood sealer
glass	clear silicone glue	eye-screws and wire into frame	create hanger
cement board	thin-set mortar	D-screws and wire	
3-D cement forms	thin-set mortar	not applicable	
terra-cotta	thin-set mortar		scratch coat of thin-set mortar

Preparing Wedi Board

Preparing wedi board is a two-part process. First you score and snap the board into the size and shape that you want, and then you tape the exposed edges with fiberglass mesh tape (which allows the edges to be grouted). The process is the same whether you're cutting a simple square or more complex shapes like the ones used in the dragonfly and hosta leaf mosaics. In the end, you'll have a completely waterproof board that is perfect for an outdoor mosaic. For safety, always wear gloves when you're applying fiberglass mesh tape.

Materials
- Wedi board
- Thin-set mortar

Tools
- Utility knife
- Gloves
- 2-in. wide fiberglass mesh tape
- Scissors

Best Use	Tiling Method	Challenges +/-	Thickness
cutting unusual shapes; versatility	all	+ easy to cut	½ in.
indoors	all	+ finish with wood frame	½ in.
large-scale panels	depends on size of work	+ can be large-scale	⅝ in.
windows	double-direct	+ transparency!	⅛-in. double-strength glass
found objects; outdoors	all	- difficult to cut	½ in. or ¼ in.
outdoors	direct	- heavy!	
accent for plantings	direct	bring indoors in winter	

PREPARING WEDI BOARD

1. Score the cement coating with a utility knife. Then, snap the board on the score line, turn the wedi over, and use a utility knife to cut through the crease on the other side.

2. Wearing gloves, wrap fiberglass mesh tape around all the exposed edges of the wedi board.

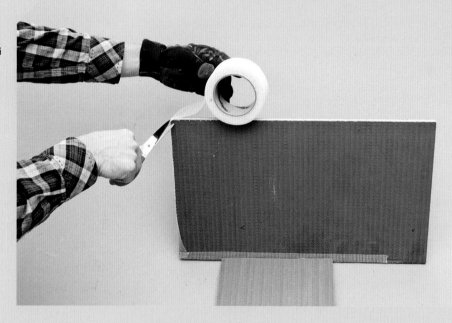

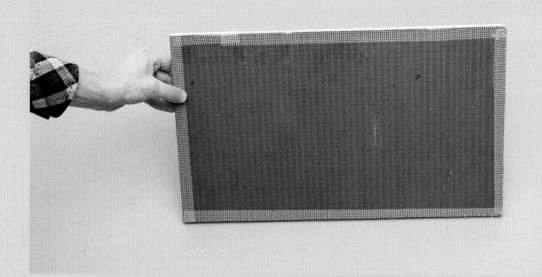

3. Still wearing gloves, fold the tape neatly around the edges, smoothing out any wrinkles, and cut it at the corners to avoid leaving wrinkles in the tape. If you're working with rounded edges, make small cuts in the tape perpendicular to the curve and layer the fiberglass mesh tape over itself so that it lies flat.

4. Spread a layer of thin-set mortar on the fiberglass mesh tape to adhere the tape to the board, as well as to give the edges a stronger skin.

Hanging Wedi Board

The one challenge to working with wedi board is installing it, because the foam core isn't strong enough to support a hanger. You can purchase specialty hanging kits from mosaic-supply retailers, or you can laminate a piece of wood onto the back of the board and screw the hanging mechanism into the wood. To do so, cut a piece of ⅜-in. plywood and glue it to the wedi board with an exterior grade construction adhesive. After the adhesive has dried, screw two small D-rings into the plywood and connect the D-rings with a wrapped wire to create a hanger. The D-ring hanger is rated to hold up to 25 pounds.

Attach a hanging device to the substrate before you begin working on the mosaic. Here, I've attached a strip of wood and a D-ring on wedi board.

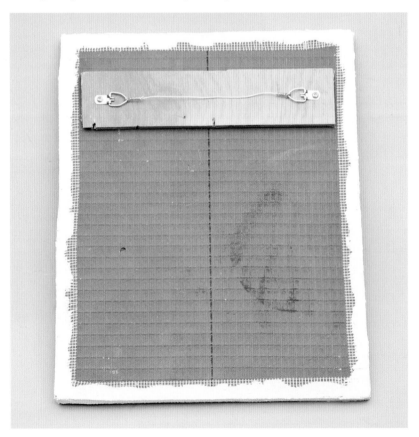

CEMENT BACKER BOARD

Strong and durable, cement backer board, such as HardieBacker, is ideal for outdoor mosaics, including tabletop mosaics. The drawback to cement backer board is that it's hard to cut, especially if you're hoping to achieve a curved substrate. A radial arm saw is best, though I've had good results using the same score-and-snap method I use with wedi board. However, be prepared to score cement backer board ten to fifteen times to achieve a score that's deep enough to snap. Cement backer board creates a lot of dust when you cut it, so wear a dust mask while you work.

Hanging Cement Backer Board

Hang cement backer board with screws and D-rings. Predrill the two holes for a tight connection, and screw in ½-in. screws. Attach D-rings to the screws and wrap a wire between them. Be sure to use short, ½-in. screws—if they're any longer, they'll poke through the front of the substrate and interfere with the mosaic.

This is a piece of cement backer board with a simple D-ring and wire hanger attached.

WOOD

Wood substrates are easy to find and set a hanger onto, and if you'd like to frame your finished mosaic, you can easily nail a frame onto the wood substrate. However, it's best to use wood only when you plan on hanging your mosaic indoors, as it's the least weather-resistant of all the substrates mentioned here. Be sure to seal all the sides of the wood first, using a 50/50 mix of PVC glue (white craft glue) and water. Simply brush on the sealant, wait for it to dry completely, and you're ready to get to work. If you want to use a wood substrate for a mosaic destined for the outdoors, then you should do one additional step to prepare the wood: use a staple gun to attach a piece of medium strength fiberglass mesh to the wood substrate. Then apply a scratch-coat layer of thin-set mortar to the fiberglass mesh and let it dry before applying the tesserae. The fiberglass mesh and thin-set will guarantee a stronger substrate for the mosaic. If you're using a wood substrate, use ⅝-in. or ¾-in. plywood for outdoors, or ½-in. medium-density fiberboard for indoors.

Hanging Wood

You can hang most wood substrates using D-rings and wire. For heavier projects (greater than 25 pounds), use French cleats. French cleats are placed horizontally across the back of the wood board, and they should span about two-thirds of the width of the board. When you're attaching the cleat, use a builder's level to make sure you are attaching the cleat straight across the board.

Both pieces of the French cleat (the one attached to the substrate and the one attached to the wall) should be predrilled in three or four places. Secure the French cleat onto the wood board using ¾-in. screws that are suitable for wood. When you're ready to hang the mosaic, measure where the companion cleat goes on the wall. Again, use a level to be sure that the cleat is hung straight across the wall.

Because of the weight of the mosaic, you'll need to screw the cleat into a wall stud or use special molly screws that can handle 25 to 50 pounds each (molly screws go into sheet rock). If you're not sure about

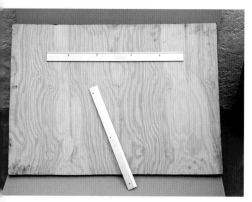

A lightweight wood substrate with D-rings and a wire attached.

For wood substrates that are heavier, use a French cleat. You'll attach one piece to the substrate and the other to the wall.

hanging, ask at a hardware store (or consult with a construction contractor or handyman) to get recommendations for hanging a heavier piece.

PRECAST CERAMIC AND CEMENT FORMS

Sometimes it's desirable to use a precast form such as a paver or a birdbath, which you can find at hardware or garden-supply stores. These are great because you can create three-dimensional mosaics, and they're immediately ready to work with—they don't require sealing or shaping before you begin the project. You can apply the adhesive and get right to work. The downside of these forms, especially cement, is that they're heavy—and will get heavier with the addition of mosaic materials—so be mindful of that factor when you're considering precast forms.

Some types of ceramic are more durable and long-lasting than others. Terra-cotta, for example, is a low-fire ceramic, which means that it's more susceptible to cracking from the pressure and moisture in freeze-thaw conditions. Most gardeners have experienced the disappointment of coming outside to find a busted terra-cotta planter, soil and roots spilling out. Imagine if you'd spent hours laboring to put a beautiful mosaic on that terra-cotta, only to find it in pieces. Spare yourself the disappointment and steer clear of low-fire ceramic. Instead, use high-fire ceramic containers, which are less porous and therefore more moisture-resistant and durable. And last, never attempt to mosaic on a glazed ceramic surface—the adhesive will not hold to the glaze.

GLASS OR ACRYLIC PLASTIC

Glass or acrylic plastic, such as Plexiglas, can be great choices for outdoor projects like bird feeders, or for mosaics you'd like to hang in the windows of your home or greenhouse. Acrylic plastic is shatterproof, so it's a safe, convenient work surface, but because it's flexible (and not rigid), it should only be used for small works—such as the bird feeder project in this book; otherwise, the grout might crack in a larger work.

If you'd like to work on glass, you can either buy new glass or recycle an old window. Secondhand windows can be found at reuse

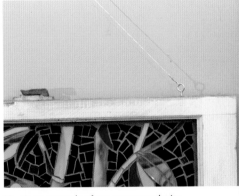

Here's an example of eye screws and wire attached to the top of a window sash. This is a detail of the Bamboo Stand on Recycled Window project.

centers or thrift stores, and they're ideal for outdoor use since they were built to be weather-resistant. If you do use an old window, be sure to clean the panes thoroughly and seal the wood frame before you get started.

Adhesives

Adhesive is used to affix the tesserae to the substrate. The type of adhesive to use depends on a combination of factors: the substrate and tesserae, and the environment in which the mosaic will live. All of the projects in this book are made using either thin-set mortar or silicone glue, because they're the most appropriate adhesives for the materials used here and for the potentially harsh weather conditions of a garden. Remember, the adhesive holds the tesserae to the substrate, but it is rarely ever visible in the finished mosaic. However, even though adhesive's role isn't aesthetic, it is crucial. Using the right adhesive is the key to making a long-lasting mosaic.

THIN-SET MORTAR

Thin-set mortar is my go-to adhesive for most mosaics destined for the outdoors, because it creates a durable, weather-resistant bond to wedi board, cement backer board, cement forms, and ceramic substrates. Thin-set mortar is a mix of cement and fine sand and is designed to adhere well in a thin layer. It can be purchased dry or premixed. A premixed thin-set, such as AcrylPro, is slightly more expensive than dry but it's a time-saver, and it's helpful to have some available when a tessera pops out of a mosaic. With premixed thin-set on hand, you can easily butter the back of the wayward tessera and set it back into the mosaic.

Preparing and Applying Thin-Set Mortar

Applying the adhesive properly is a key factor in a mosaic. Application methods vary slightly according to which working method you use to seat the tesserae—direct or double-direct—but the general directions here are a good foundation. The trick to applying adhesive properly is to learn just how much to lay—if you apply too much the adhesive might squish up between the tesserae and interfere with the grouting process later. It takes a little practice to get it just right, but it's another aspect of mosaic that can be mastered with time.

Materials
- Thin-set mortar, dry or premixed

Tools
- Notched metal trowel
- Flat mixing trowel
- Small bucket for mixing dry thin-set
- Small pitcher of water
- Dust mask

If you're using a pre-mixed thin-set, you can skip steps 1 and 2.

1. **Measure the thin-set mortar.** Put on a dust mask. In a small mixing bowl, measure out one cup (8 oz.) of dry thin-set per square foot of mosaic.

2. **Mix the thin-set mortar.** Add one part water to three parts dry thin-set bit by bit, using a flat mixing trowel to mix the thin-set, until it reaches a consistency that is thin but not runny. Let the thin-set slake for ten minutes (slaking is a chemical activation process that gives the thin-set its holding power). Once the thin-set has slaked, it is active for up to 90 minutes—after that, you have to throw it out. (To make it last longer, you can store it in a lidded container or zippered sandwich bag while you're working.) Once the thin-set has slaked, you cannot add more dry thin-set or water to it, because any additions will disrupt the chemical process that occurred during slaking. If you find yourself needing more thin-set, which often happens, you must mix up a new batch.

Dispose of leftover thin-set mortar in a garbage can—not in a drain, because it will clog the pipe. To clean your trowels, scrape away the excess thin-set and sponge them off completely in a bucket of water. Then, throw the dirty water out on the cement outside.

A notched trowel leaves a bed that has a tooth, or grain. The wet thin-set will naturally shift as you press a tessera into it. The grooves in the toothed bed create some space so that thin-set doesn't squish out from under the tesserae and block the grout lines.

3. **Apply the thin-set to the substrate.** Using the flat mixing trowel, scoop a dollop of adhesive onto the surface of the substrate. Then, using a notched trowel, spread the adhesive in an even layer, holding the trowel at a 45-degree angle and pressing the tooth of the trowel firmly against the substrate (you should be able to hear the scratch); this lets the teeth drag through the thin-set and create a notched surface. Move quickly through this stage so the thin-set doesn't dry.

4. **Seat your tesserae.** How you seat your tesserae will depend on the working method—direct or double direct. While the thin-set is still wet and active, seat the tesserae by pressing them down firmly into the thin-set to ensure full coverage on their back sides. Use a small folded-up cloth to push each tile into place.

   At this point, you'll be able to see whether you applied the right amount of thin-set. Ideally, when you push a tessera down, you should see a small quantity of thin-set squish out from beneath—but not so much that it rises above the surface level of the tesserae. If it does, you used too much. But practice makes perfect, so you'll get a better sense of how much to apply as you continue making mosaics.

   After seating the tesserae, apply an even weight on top (if the mosaic has a flat surface, that is; otherwise, skip it). I use a bin of broken glass as a weight, but a large book (or books) would work well, too.

5. **Let the thin-set mortar dry.** For the best results, let the thin-set mortar dry overnight, preferably for 24 hours. Once the thin-set is dry, you're ready to move on to the next step of the mosaic process—grouting, which you'll read about in Grouting Your Mosaic.

If you're adding a mosaic to just a portion of a substrate, it's helpful to apply a scratch coat of thin-set to the area. A scratch coat gives you an outline of the mosaic, which helps ensure that you stay within the outline when you're seating the tesserae. If you're not sure if a surface is adequate for adhering tesserae, a scratch coat can improve the surface of a substrate (as shown in the Jeweled Frog Planter on page 210) and provide additional durability to the finished piece. Let the scratch coat cure for 24 hours before applying the next coat of thin-set.

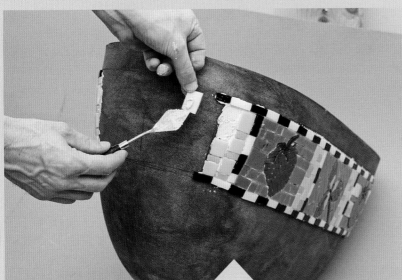

Use a small trowel to butter the back of a tessera with thin-set mortar before hand-setting it into the scratch coat.

For neat and efficient application of thin-set mortar, make a do-it-yourself piping bag. Fill a strong plastic sandwich bag with thin-set and cut off a small piece of one corner. Hold the bag in one hand, pick up a tessera with the other, and use the bag to apply thin-set to the tessera. A piping bag allows you to work quickly in the direct method.

CLEAR SILICONE GLUE

Because it's colorless, clear silicone glue is excellent for glass-on-glass. One of the aesthetic advantages of a glass or acrylic-plastic substrate is that the sun can shine through the mosaic, creating a pleasing interplay of light and color. If you were to use thin-set mortar for such a project, its opacity would block the sunlight.

In addition to glass-on-glass or glass-on-acrylic-plastic projects, silicone glue is excellent for affixing mirrored tiles to any substrate—other adhesives will corrode the mirror's reflective backing.

Applying Silicone Glue

Before you apply silicone glue to glass or acrylic plastic, be sure to clean the surface with glass cleaner to remove any debris that might impede the glue. When I'm applying silicone glue to glass or acrylic plastic, I typically use a small, 3-in. wide piece of straight-edge matte board as a trowel. The board is sturdy yet flexible, which results in an even application of glue, and it can be discarded after use. Silicone has a strong odor, so either work outdoors or in a well-ventilated room.

Materials
- Clear silicone glue with caulk gun
- Glass substrate
- Matte board, 3 × 2-in. piece with a straight edge

ADHESIVE VS. GROUT Adhesive is the mortar or glue that affixes the tesserae to the substrate. It's rarely visible in the final mosaic, since it's usually hidden beneath the tesserae and grout. Most grouts, on the other hand, have no adhesive properties. Grout fills the interstices, or spaces, between tesserae, offering overall stability and weatherproofing, and it contributes to the aesthetics of the finished design.

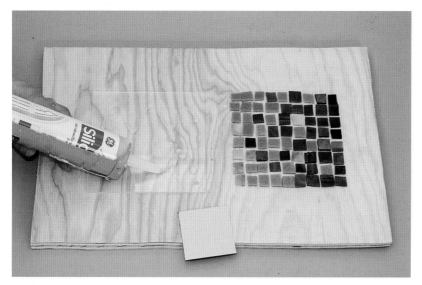

1. **Squirt silicone onto the surface of the substrate.** There's no way to truly measure the amount of silicone you'll need, but a good rule of thumb is to put down one squiggle line every three inches, as shown here.

2. **Spread the silicone.** Using a small straight-edge matte board, gently smooth the silicone across the surface of the substrate in a thin, even layer all the way to the edges. Work quickly before the glue becomes tacky and difficult to spread.

3. **Check the coverage.** Hold the substrate up to the light to see if you've achieved an even, thorough coverage of silicone glue. Working with silicone glue takes some practice—if you apply too much, it'll squish up above the tesserae. If you apply too little, you'll have some loose tesserae. If you discover any loose tesserae later, simply pop them out and re-glue them.

Grouts

Whereas adhesive affixes the tesserae to the substrate, grout fills the gaps—also called interstices or joints—between them. Although most grouts have no adhesive properties, they strengthen the mosaic physically, add to its water-resistance, and create a cohesive finished piece. Plus, grout adds an artistic element of line to the piece, and your choice of grout color affects the overall design.

The two grouts that I recommend are cementitious grout and urethane grout. I recommend working with cementitious grout on most of the projects in this book because it's durable and easy to use. However, once you become comfortable using cementitious grout, you might try using urethane grout for its built-in adhesive and sealant.

CEMENTITIOUS GROUT

Cementitious grout is the usual choice for mosaic projects, because it's durable, easy to work with, and can be colored to complement your design choices. For the most part, you can do any mosaic project with cementitious grout—it's the standard grout of the tiling trade. Cementitious grout comes sanded or unsanded. I prefer sanded, because it gives me the flexibility to make wider grout lines when I want them.

URETHANE GROUT

Urethane grout is stronger than cementitious grout because it has a built-in adhesive and sealant. It's an excellent choice for mosaics that will get a lot of use, such as birdbaths, fountains, and all-weather tabletops. It's sold in a premix form, which eliminates the need to mix and slake it, but it's harder to apply and clean than cementitious grout. The adhesive in urethane grout dries somewhat quickly, so you have a shorter timeframe for applying it.

Grouting Your Mosaic

When you mix grout, be sure to wear a dust mask to avoid breathing in the fine particles. Grout is activated by water, and the inside of your nose, mouth, and lungs are moist environments.

Materials

- Cementitious grout
- Grout sealant

Tools

- Medium-size bowl
- Flat mixing trowel
- Rubber grout float for spreading grout
- Cotton cloths for polishing the finished mosaic
- Small sponge for shaping grouted shoulders
- Small bucket of water
- Dust mask

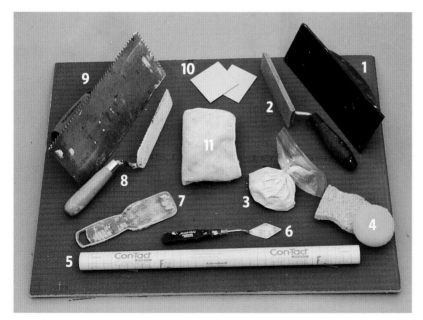

Tools for mixing and applying grout and adhesives.

1. Rubber grout float
2. Margin grout float
3. Sandwich bag adhesive dispenser
4. Sponges
5. Clear contact paper
6. Metal painter's trowel
7. Plastic mixing trowel
8. Margin notched trowel (for adhesive)
9. Notched trowel (for adhesive)
10. Matte boards (for applying silicone glue)
11. Cotton cloth (for polishing during grout process)

It's always a good idea to have some ready-made thin-set mortar on hand while you're grouting your mosaic. If a tessera becomes dislodged, you can butter the back of it with the mortar and gently reset it during the grouting process—you won't have to stop to prepare the mortar.

1. **Mix the grout.** Measure the amount of dry grout you'll need—approximately six ounces of dry grout per square foot of mosaic—into a bowl. On the side, have a bucket of water ready. Before adding water to the grout, use the flat mixing trowel to stir the dry grout to break up any chunks. The grout should be very fine. Then, slowly add water to the grout, a little at a time. You'll use an approximate ratio of three parts grout to one part water, but it's best to add the water bit by bit. Stir the mixture thoroughly until it's thick but still fluid. Test the consistency of the grout by holding up a dollop on your mixing trowel; the grout should hold to the trowel but eventually slide off slowly. If the grout holds to the trowel steadily, it might be too thick; if it drips off, it's too thin.

Before you begin grouting, test the weight of the grout. Here, the grout is holding on the mixing trowel, so it's the right consistency.

2. **Let the grout slake.** After you've mixed the grout, let it slake by leaving it undisturbed for ten minutes. Once the grout has slaked, it will be active for two to three hours; after that, you'll need to throw it out. Break up the slaked grout with a trowel and stir it to an even consistency. While you're working you can break up the grout and stir it again to reconstitute it, but do not add water. If you find that you didn't prepare enough grout, mix more—but don't forget to let it slake.

3. **Apply the grout to the mosaic.** Grouting a mosaic takes about 30 minutes per square foot, including grouting the edges. Before you apply the grout, elevate the mosaic, if possible. Elevating the mosaic allows you to access the edges of the piece more easily and grout them without creating a mess on your worktable.

I've elevated the mosaic on a plastic tub to make it easier to access the edges and to avoid getting grout on my work surface.

First, grout the surface of the mosaic. Drop a blob of grout onto the middle of the mosaic and, using a rubber grout float, spread the grout in all directions so that it fills every channel. While you're working, pull the grout float *toward you* to spread the grout rather than push it away from you, which can dislodge a tile.

Once you've grouted the entire surface, pull any excess grout into the middle of the mosaic. This will give you the visibility you need to check for any cavities that still need to be filled and to make sure the grout is evenly applied. If you see any inconsistencies, fill them now.

Next, grout the shoulder, or edges, of the mosaic. The shoulder is the ⅛-in. border between the edge of the mosaic and the edge of the substrate that you left when you made the mosaic. Wipe some grout into the shoulder. Hold the grout float at an angle to apply the grout to the shoulders. The shoulders should be grouted uniformly, but don't worry about making them perfect—you'll sculpt the shoulders later with a sponge. When you're done grouting the edges, you shouldn't be able to see the substrate.

Finally, hold your trowel at an angle and do a final sweep across the entire mosaic to pull off any excess grout—this will help minimize cleanup later. Let the grouted mosaic sit undisturbed for about 15 minutes.

The edges of your mosaic will be fragile for a day or two until the grout fully cures, so be careful not to hold your mosaic by the edges.

4. **Contour the edges of the mosaic.** Begin by soaking a clean sponge in water. Squeeze the sponge thoroughly until it's damp but not dripping, because you don't want to add any water to the drying grout. Lightly run the sponge along the edges of the mosaic. You're merely softening and evening the edges. At this time, you can smooth out any rough spots, or add a touch more grout to any barren spots. In the end, the edges of the mosaic should be flush with the surface and appear relatively smooth. As you work, rinse and squeeze your sponge as needed to clean off any grout that it picks up.

5. **Apply the sprinkle coat of grout.** A sprinkling of dry grout over the surface of the mosaic speeds up the drying process by absorbing moisture, and it provides grit for polishing the mosaic. As a rule of thumb, don't begin this step until at least an hour after you've begun the grouting process. Gently sprinkle a fine coating of dry grout across the surface of the piece. Wait five minutes. Then, using a dry cotton cloth, angle your mosaic toward the trash can and, being mindful not to create too much dust, wipe off the bulk of the dry grout into a trash can.

A light coat of grout sprinkled on the mosaic helps speed up the drying process.

6. **Polish the surface.** This is the exciting part! Use a dry cotton cloth to remove the remaining grout from the surface of your mosaic. Polish in a circular motion, thoroughly cleaning the surface of every tessera. When you're working on the edge of the mosaic, make sure to wipe toward the center, being mindful not to disturb the grouting at the edge. It's normal to see a "grout haze" form even after polishing; you can remove this haze by simply coming back to your mosaic in the next three hours and repolishing the surface.

7. **Seal your mosaic.** For added durability against the elements, you should seal your mosaic with grout sealant. (This applies to cementitious grout only.) To do so, wait 48 hours for the grout to cure completely. You can then use a paintbrush or sponge to apply the sealant according to the manufacturer's instructions. Once you layer on the sealant, wait 20 minutes for it to dry, and then polish the surface of the mosaic with a dry cloth. The sealant only seals the grout—it won't stain the glass.

Dispose of leftover grout in a garbage can—not in a drain. (It will clog the drain.) To clean your floats, scrape away the excess grout and sponge the floats off completely in a bucket of water. Then, throw the dirty water out on the cement outside.

Mosaic Design Basics

Though you are welcome to re-create the templates and design schemes I use for the projects in this book, you will undoubtedly find yourself wanting to branch out and create designs to complement your own garden. A few basic concepts will help you on your way toward creating mosaics with a pleasing balance of colors, shapes, and patterns.

Cartoon

A cartoon is the full-size sketch, or template, of the design for your mosaic. It doesn't have to be detailed—it should be a simplified rendition of the design and leave plenty of room for spontaneity. You can see that some of the projects shown here ended up differing slightly from the template that appears at the back of the book. In part, the beauty of mosaic is in the serendipity of tile shapes, which you can't plan for. The most important elements of the cartoon are the outline and the clear separation of the subject matter and the background. If you include too much detail in your cartoon, you'll hamper your ability to go with the flow when an interesting tessera shows up in your bank. Also, keep in mind that the grout lines are only one of several elements that make a mosaic. You also have shape, color, pattern, and texture to work with. So while your cartoon might seem very simple, rest assured that the finished piece will be rich and interesting.

Here's a real hosta leaf along with the simple drawing I made for the cartoon.

DRAWING OBJECTS

The more you mosaic, the more you'll find yourself stumbling upon objects that you'd like to translate into a design. For example, I found a hosta leaf in my garden and decided it would make a beautiful mosaic (see page 111). Here are a few tips to help you translate an idea into a cartoon.

1. **Draw an outline of the object.** Using a pencil (so you can make changes), draw a basic outline of the object. Don't get too hung up on the various contours; you'll use color—not line—to create a sense of contour. If you like, darken the line by going over it with a felt-tip marker.

2. **Add color.** Use colored pencils or watercolors to add color to the drawing. I added the lightest values of yellow and followed with darker values of green, layering in additional yellows and greens. The more I looked at this hosta leaf, the more values I saw.

The dark lines represent the grout lines. The colored areas represent the tesserae.

Using watercolors, I layered in the green hues—first the light and then the dark.

Here, I scaled up a 4 × 6-in. design by a multiple of 3 into a 12 × 18-in. cartoon, using the lines of the axes as reference points.

SCALING YOUR CARTOON TO SIZE

If you're experimenting with a design, an easy way to do so is with thumbnails—small, quick sketches. This gives you the freedom to make several drawings until you're satisfied with the composition. Then, you can scale up the thumbnail to fit your substrate. When you're conceptualizing the piece, you'll need to use a shape similar to the finished size. For example, you can scale up a 4×6-in. drawing by multiples of three, into a 12×18-in. cartoon. (If you are using a template from the back of this book, scale it up as you would for your own cartoon.)

The scaled cartoon should fit on the substrate, with a border of at least $\frac{1}{8}$-in. between the edge of the cartoon and the edge of the substrate in order to leave enough space for a shoulder that will be grouted later. A sufficient shoulder is imperative for the overall strength of the mosaic. Here are three methods for scaling your cartoon to size:

1. **Draw the design to scale.** Draw the design directly onto a sheet of paper that is approximately the same size as the substrate you plan to mosaic.

2. **Scale the cartoon with a photocopier.** This is a good way to work with the templates in this book.

3. **Scale the cartoon by hand.** This method is easiest to understand with an example. If the thumbnail sketch is 4×6 in. and the substrate is 12×18 in., then the thumbnail needs to be increased by a factor of three ($3 \times 4 = 12$; $3 \times 6 = 18$).

Draw a horizontal axis and a vertical axis through the center of the thumbnail sketch. Draw corresponding axes on the larger sheet of paper. Both sheets of paper should now be divided into four equal boxes, and the axes that you drew will be your reference points as you create a new, larger drawing. Each box has unique information, and as you draw you'll focus on one box at a time. Working on one box, draw the design that

In *opus regulatum*, tesserae of similar size and shape are lined up in a grid fashion. The border of the labyrinth mosaic is a good example of *opus regulatum*.

you see in the thumbnail in the corresponding box on the larger sheet of paper. Note where your drawing crosses the lines dividing the boxes on the thumbnail. Mark those spots on the axes on the larger sheet of paper to ensure that the lines of your drawing pass through them at the corresponding places. Moving from box to box, draw only what you see in the box you're working on, focusing particularly on matching up the lines of the drawing that meet along the axes. Then fill in the interior lines once you've captured the outlines.

If you're working on a much larger substrate, you can break the thumbnail sketch and the cartoon into more boxes to give yourself more reference points.

Opus

In mosaic, the word *opus* (or *opera*, for the plural form) refers to the way the pattern of the tiles is worked. There are six *opera*, each of which involves laying tesserae in a particular pattern. Each *opus* creates its own distinct effect in a piece, and you can create a mosaic in one *opus*, or mix and match *opera* within a single mosaic.

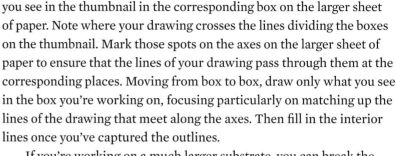

Opus tessellatum is similar to *opus regulatum*, except that alternating rows are staggered like brickwork.

Opus palladianum is a free-flowing style in which tesserae of random shape and size are laid in an irregular pattern as they are in the green area here.

In *opus vermiculatum*, the subject of the mosaic is outlined with a border of tesserae.

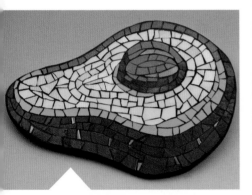

Opus musivum builds on *opus vermiculatum*, extending the subject's border out to the edge of the mosaic.

In *opus sectile*, objects are formed with a single large tessera—rather than being composed of many small tesserae.

Andamento

Andamento is the organization of the tesserae that gives the mosaic its flow and sense of order. It's a feeling you can create in the piece based on how you choose to orient the tesserae. A mosaic with *andamento* can create a very satisfying effect for viewers. A brick wall is a good example of horizontal *andamento*—the horizontal grout lines are unbroken, which leads the eye, while the vertical grout lines are broken up. A creative way to visualize *andamento* is to imagine a multilane highway filled with cars. The cars are the tesserae and the *andamento* flows in the direction of the lanes.

Here are three good examples of *andamento*. The first is the flamelike hair used in the Chimenea mosaic, the second is the Tulip Mosaic with Plant Box, and the third is the Spiral Stepping-Stone.

Tessellation

To tessellate means to create a repeated pattern using tesserae that fit uniformly next to each other. Our eyes love patterns, and tessellated mosaics mimic the organic patterns in plants, making tessellation ideal for garden mosaics. You can tessellate an entire mosaic or just a part of it, such as a border.

Here's an example of tessellation on the border of the Round Tabletop mosaic.

Color: Hue and Value

Color theory is a vast subject, but when you're designing a mosaic, you should focus on the basics of hue and value.

Hue is color in its pure form, which you've likely seen represented by a color wheel. When you're choosing a color scheme for your mosaic, it's important to remember that the colors will be working in relation to each other. You can work with harmonious colors (colors that are *next* to each other on the color wheel) or complementary colors (colors that are *across* from each other on the color wheel). You can mix and match your color selection depending on the overall effect you're hoping to achieve.

Before committing to your color scheme, shade in your cartoon with colored pencils or watercolors.

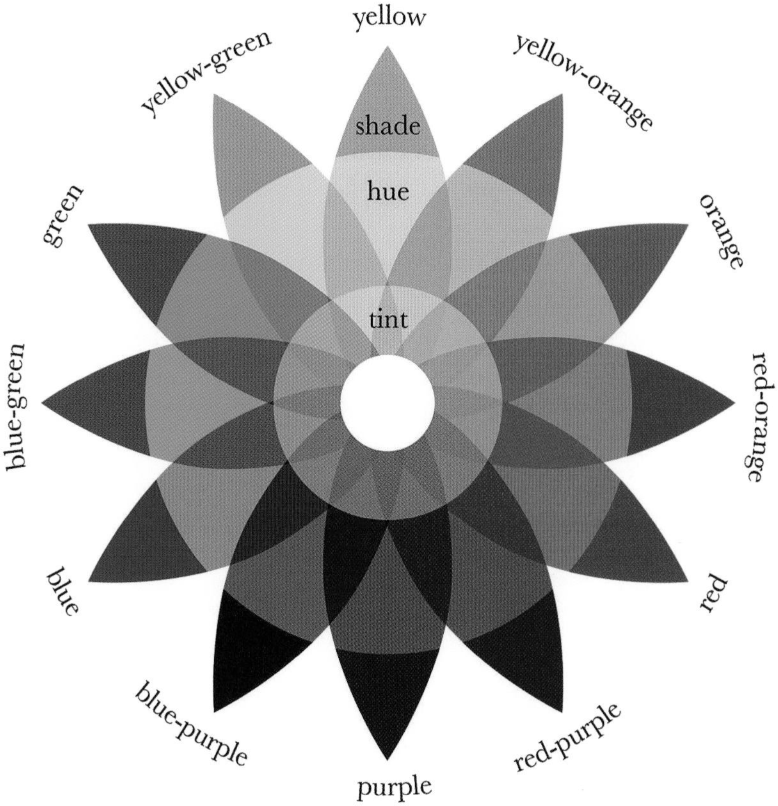

The color wheel can help you choose harmonious or complementary colors.

The color wheel diagram with labels: yellow, yellow-green, yellow-orange, green, orange, blue-green, red-orange, blue, red, blue-purple, red-purple, purple. Inner labels: shade, hue, tint.

For example, perhaps you're making a mosaic featuring a flower against a background of sky. If you're using blue for the sky and green for the leaves—harmonious colors, because they're next to each other on the color wheel—you would then want to choose a complementary color, like red or orange, for the petals, which will make them pop by comparison.

When I'm using color in mosaic, I always try to control the chaos. With so many color choices available, I try to limit the variety so that there's not a fight for the viewer's attention. Instead, I choose colors that will work together to create something larger.

You can change the value of a color by adding black or white to the basic hue. Though value is a less obvious trait than hue, it's equally important when considering a color scheme for your mosaic. Value affects the sense of depth. A shadowed area calls for darker values, while a highlight on an object calls for a lighter value. This contrast will help to separate different areas of the mosaic. A dark blue will recede while a light blue comes forward. The key is to have contrasting values where necessary.

For instance, let's continue the example of the flower mosaic. Though blue and green are different colors, it's possible that they can have the same value, depending on how much black or white is in their respective compositions. If values are too similar, it's difficult to distinguish between them at a glance. If the blue and green are of the same value, your viewer will have trouble visually separating the leaves from the sky.

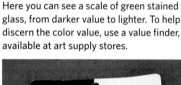

Here you can see a scale of green stained glass, from darker value to lighter. To help discern the color value, use a value finder, available at art supply stores.

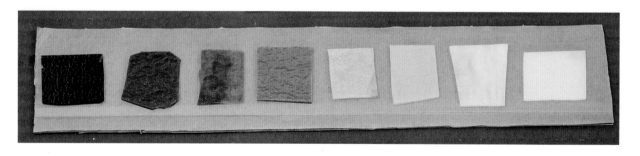

To avoid this visual muddling, choose a green and a blue with varying values. A sky blue (blue plus white) will have a lighter value, while a forest green (green plus black) will have a darker value. You can create the flower mosaic with forest green leaves and a sky blue background, and their contrasting values will let the viewer clearly discern the sky from the leaves.

There is an easy way to check whether you have a successful mix of values. Once you've dry laid the mosaic, take a black-and-white photo of it with a digital camera or smartphone. When you look at the photo, it will be immediately clear whether there's a pleasing amount of contrast—you'll see plenty of exaggerated dark and light areas in the photo. If you took a photo of the flower mosaic, you'd be able to see immediately whether the blue and green were of different enough values that they are separate to the eye.

Here the green leaves and the blue sky have contrasting values.

White grout brightens this mosaic.

Dark grout unifies the background of the Labyrinth mosaic, allowing the background to recede and giving prominence to the labyrinth itself.

Grout: Interstices and Color

Though it may seem like a humble element of a mosaic, grout holds a piece together, both structurally and visually. When laying tesserae, be mindful of the width and uniformity of the interstices—they will affect the overall coherence of the mosaic. If the interstices are very wide, or if they are wildly uneven, the finished effect will be fragmented visually. If you take another look at the *operas* described earlier, you'll notice that the interstices are just as important as the tesserae in creating the desired effect of the *opus*.

Common choices for grout color are white and gray, though you can purchase colored grout from a hardware or craft store. Gray is a good choice because of its neutral value, which is why you'll see gray grout featured in many of the mosaics in this book. Earth tones are likewise excellent for natural subjects and will be a harmonious fit for a garden. White grout adds brightness to a mosaic, but it shows dirt and highlights inconsistent grout lines. If you use white grout, be sure to apply a sealant to protect it from becoming dingy.

The red-brown grout lends a sense of earthiness to the Found Objects mosaic.

Ocean blue grout complements the many greens in the Hosta Leaf mosaic.

The Mosaic Process: Direct, Double-Direct, and Reverse Methods

The projects in this book feature three working methods for seating tesserae: direct, double-direct, and reverse. The working method used in a given mosaic project depends on variables such as substrate, tesserae type, and the overall size and weight of the project. For complex projects, I find that I use a combination of methods to complete the work. Try working with the methods recommended for each project until you find the methods that work most comfortably for you.

Direct Method

The direct method is what people typically envision when they think of mosaic. In the direct method, you simply use an adhesive to apply each individual tessera directly to the substrate. The greatest advantage to this method is that it's straightforward, and you can see your design face-up and track your progress as you work. It's imperative to use the direct method when you mosaic a three-dimensional object such as a precast cement form. However, using the direct method is akin to doing a crossword puzzle with a pen. You have to be confident that you're not going to want to make changes. Also, when you work piece by piece, it can be easy to lose sight of the overall composition. Be thorough with your design and planning so that you figure out the details beforehand and aren't met with any surprises during the process.

For instructions and photographs illustrating working in the direct method, see the Round Tabletop (page 147) and Pagoda (page 215) mosaics.

Double-Direct Method

Double-direct is the method you'll use for most of the projects in this book. It's *direct* in that you can see your design face-up and track your progress while you work. However, you are not actually adhering the tesserae to the substrate as you work. Instead, you lay your tesserae on a piece of sticky mesh that's placed on the cartoon, and then, once you've finalized the composition, you transfer it to the substrate in its entirety. The sticky mesh creates a secure work surface, but it still allows you a lot of wiggle room to rearrange and swap out tiles while you work.

When you're working in the double-direct method, always begin the same way—by *dry laying* the tesserae on the sticky mesh. From there, though, the setting technique varies according to the size and shape of your substrate. We'll cover three different techniques: flip-and-set, drape-and-set, and double-direct-with-slide. Flipping, draping, and sliding your mosaic may sound like nerve-wracking propositions, but rest assured that your composition will be secure.

For in-depth instructions on the double-direct method, see the Address Sign project (page 73).

Reverse Method

The reverse method varies significantly from the direct and double-direct methods. It's a fairly simple technique that's been in use for centuries and might even seem primitive in comparison to some of the highly complex mosaics you see nowadays. Today we have the advantage of technologies that weren't available centuries ago when the reverse method was invented. Nonetheless, it's intriguing to revisit the old ways of doing things.

Using the reverse method, the mosaic is created upside down, so you're looking at the back side of the mosaic as you work. (I know, it sounds a little crazy!) Why would you work with your tesserae upside down, where you can't see the finished surface of your design? Because it allows you to put the adhesive directly on the back side of the tesserae without having to move anything. In the Pebble Stepping-Stone project, concrete is poured onto the back side of the pebbles. The concrete acts as an adhesive, and a concrete paver is created in one fell swoop. It's an interesting twist on mosaic.

For more instructions on the reverse method, see the Pebble Stepping-Stone mosaic (page 195).

MOSAIC PROJECTS

An address mosaic lends a personal touch to your home.

Address Sign

EASY

Start here! If you're new to mosaic, I highly recommend beginning with this project. It will give you a strong foundation in the basic how-to steps that you'll find in many of the other projects in this book, especially those that use the double-direct method.

A handmade address sign is a cheerful addition to your home, and you can customize the colors and design to complement your house, garden, and personal style. A mosaic address sign makes a lovely housewarming gift, too.

When you design an address sign, bear in mind that visibility and readability are crucial if you want it to be functional. Use a substrate that is rectangular or oval and measures approximately 10 × 18 inches. These dimensions provide enough space for the numbers to be clearly presented and also leave enough room for aesthetic touches for visual interest. The numbers should be at least four inches tall, and you should use a number style that is clean and legible. To differentiate the numbers, be sure to leave ample room between them and space them evenly apart. To make the numbers stand out from the background, it's wise to use a contrasting value of color—dark for the numbers and light for the background. When you're ready to hang the address sign, make sure you choose a spot with a dedicated light source so that it's visible at night.

Once you've settled the practicalities, spend some time thinking about the aesthetics of the address sign. For this project, I decided to

Materials

- Prepared wedi board, approximately 10 × 18 in., with hanger attached
- Cartoon
- Gloves
- Fiberglass mesh tape
- Sticky mesh
- Clear contact paper
- Stained glass
- Thin-set mortar
- Cementitious grout
- Grout sealant

Tools

- Pistol-grip glass cutter
- Glass runner
- Two-wheeled nipper
- Dust mask
- Felt-tip marker
- Painter's tape
- Bowl
- Flat mixing trowel
- Notched metal trowel
- Small painter's trowel
- Rubber grout float
- Cotton cloths
- Sponge
- Bucket

Templates, pages 268, 269

use a flowered panel and a complementary green border. I chose the green hues not only because they're pleasing, but also because they offer contrast to the mosaic's white background and they won't impede the readability of the address.

When you select your color scheme, remember to take into account the color of your house. If your house is a neutral color, like the one in the photo, then you'll want to use a contrasting color scheme so that the mosaic doesn't blend in with the house paint.

1. **Secure the cartoon and sticky mesh to the substrate.** Your cartoon should fit on the substrate, with a border of at least 1/8 in. between the edge of the cartoon and the edge of the substrate in order to leave enough space for a shoulder that will be grouted later. Lay the cartoon face-up on the prepared substrate and place sticky mesh—sticky side up—on top of the cartoon. If the sticky mesh inhibits your view of the design, use a marker to darken the lines of the cartoon. Then, tape down the corners with painter's tape to affix the cartoon and sticky mesh to the substrate so that your work surface and design will be secure and properly aligned while you lay the tesserae.

2. **Dry lay the tesserae.** Dry lay the entire composition directly on the sticky mesh over the cartoon. When you get to the corners, remove the painter's tape so that the tesserae can properly adhere to the sticky mesh. Finalize the design at this stage and check the borders to ensure that no tesserae have crept over the edges of the cartoon. If they have, switch them out for smaller pieces to avoid creating a sharp edge or an insufficient shoulder for grouting.

Laying tesserae is a very forgiving process, as you typically start with a *dry lay*, meaning that you first arrange the tesserae on a dry substrate. This gives you the freedom to make changes to the design until you're happy with it. Then, you affix the tesserae to the substrate with adhesive.

Here's an example of a vertical address mosaic. It doesn't include aesthetic embellishments like the flower in this project, but the red and white color scheme gives it excellent readability.

3. **Cover the composition with contact paper.** Take a sheet of contact paper, slightly larger than the composition, and gently place it—sticky side down—on the surface of the mosaic, locking all the tesserae in place. Press the contact paper firmly onto each and every tessera, being mindful of the sharp edges under the contact paper. To avoid cutting yourself, use a balled-up cloth to press the tesserae down.

4. **Remove the composition from the substrate.** Before you can apply adhesive to the substrate, you must first remove the cartoon and sticky mesh from its surface. The easiest way to do this is with the aid of a flipper board—a board that you use to flip the composition over. The board can be any flat, lightweight board you have on hand—a spare piece of wood, plastic, or wedi board. As long as it's slightly larger than your mosaic, it will work.

continued on page 80

Here, you can see the cartoon and sticky mesh taped to the substrate as I dry lay the tesserae.

I've begun adding an artistic border to the mosaic. I used a medium-value sage green for the background, so I chose a darker green for the flower stem to create a high contrast of values.

I created flow in this piece by outlining the stem with a border of tesserae (*opus vermiculatum*). I added visual variety by using long, curved pieces in the flower panel, whereas the uppermost part of the design is just straight cuts.

TIPS FOR LAYING TESSERAE

- Lay the principle subject matter first, then the background. If your mosaic design includes a border, lay those pieces before filling in the interior of the background.
- Lay custom shapes first. Then, surround them with tesserae from your bank. It's easier to fill in around a custom shape.
- Be mindful of the interstices. The interstices are the gaps between the tesserae. Be sure to leave enough room between the tesserae to apply an adequate amount of grout. For the overall continuity of the mosaic, try to make all interstices the same width.
- Create *andamento*. If possible, try to create flow within the piece by deliberately organizing the tesserae and grout lines.
- Be flexible. The beauty of mosaic is in the variety of shapes that come together to make the whole. Try not to get too hung up on getting an exact shape or size for each tessera.

The surface of the mosaic is covered with clear contact paper to secure the tesserae. The board on top will serve as the flipper board.

Here the mosaic is reversed, sitting on the flipper board. The cartoon and sticky mesh have been removed, but the contact paper is still adhered to the front of the mosaic.

To avoid cutting yourself on sharp edges, press the tesserae down through the contact paper using a balled-up cloth.

Here, the tesserae have been seated into the thin-set mortar, and the contact paper has been removed. I used white mortar for this project, which is great for a glass-tesserae mosaic because it brightens up the colors from below.

continued from page 75

To safely remove your composition, place the flipper board on top of it. Hold both the top and bottom boards (the bottom being the substrate) securely—with the tesserae sandwiched safely in between—and simply flip them over. After you've executed the flip, your substrate will be on top of the pile. Remove it and face it right-side up on your work surface.

5. **Remove the cartoon and sticky mesh.** Remove the cartoon and gently pull the sticky mesh off the tesserae, being careful to pull slowly to avoid dislodging any tesserae from the contact paper underneath. As I say to my students, "pull it low and slow." Discard the sticky mesh.

6. **Apply thin-set mortar to the substrate.** Now that your substrate is bare, it's ready for adhesive. When you're working in the double-direct method on a relatively small substrate like this, apply adhesive to the entire substrate at once. Follow the directions in Preparing and Applying Thin-Set Mortar on page 42.

7. **Flip-and-set the composition back onto the substrate.** Now that the substrate is covered with adhesive, transfer the composition to the substrate and seat the tesserae all at once. Keep in mind that, because you flipped the mosaic, you're looking at the back side of the composition now.

There are a few different techniques for transferring your design, depending on the size, shape, and weight of the substrate. Here, we use the flip-and-set technique. This maneuver requires that you pick up the substrate, so it's best suited for small mosaics that are done on a lightweight substrate (such as wedi board).

Pick up your substrate. Turn it over and hold it upside-down so that the side covered with thin-set mortar faces down. Measuring with your eyes, align the substrate with the composition, and then gently lay the substrate down on the composition. Don't worry about perfecting the alignment just yet.

Next, press the entire piece together, holding the top and bottom boards firmly, and flip them over. Remove the flipper board and set it aside. Now you can see your mosaic face-up. If necessary, center the mosaic by pulling the corners of the contact paper with both hands. It's fun to see the mosaic move as a unit.

8. **Seat the tesserae.** Smooth down the entire composition through the contact paper, pressing each tessera into the thin-set mortar to ensure adhesion. Use a balled-up cloth during this process to avoid cutting yourself on any sharp edges. Place an even weight (such as a book) on the top of the mosaic to help the setting process, and let the mortar begin to cure for approximately 30 minutes. After 30 minutes, gently lift a corner of the contact paper. If you feel confident that you can pull away the contact paper without pulling up any tesserae, do so. The mortar will still be wet at this point, so if necessary you can do some final fine-tuning to the mosaic design.

9. **Clean up any extra adhesive.** The adhesive will be visible in the interstices. This is a problem only if it has squished up between the tesserae so much that it might block the grout. A good way to check for problem spots is to look at the contact paper after you pull it off—if it's spotted with mortar, the adhesive has risen above the level of the tesserae. If you see any problem spots, clean them out using a small painter's trowel or a thin piece of wire. Then let the thin-set mortar cure for 24 hours.

10. **Grout, polish, and seal the mosaic.** Follow the directions in Grouting Your Mosaic on page 49.

Turn your favorite tree into a gathering space for feathered friends.

Bird Feeder

EASY

Hanging a bird feeder from a tree or the eaves is a perfect way to draw life and sound to your garden no matter the season. Nothing beats waking up to the merry chirping of birds as they feast on the buffet of birdseed you've provided, courtesy of a beautifully crafted mosaic bird feeder.

I purchased a bird feeder from a local garden-supply store. It has a removable acrylic plastic panel, which is perfect for using glass tiles on. I used stained-glass tesserae, adhered with clear silicone glue, so that the sun can shine through the composition.

When a substrate is small, like this one, it's important to keep the design simple. For this project, a simple design also helps give more impact to the bird in the mosaic. Of course, you'll want to replicate the basic shape of a bird, but remember to balance that with the challenge of cutting tiles in unusual shapes. I cut larger tesserae for the bird and smaller tesserae for the background. This brings the bird forward in the viewer's eye, making it the focal point of the mosaic.

When you're working with glass-on-acrylic-plastic, try to create an interplay between translucent and opaque stained glass. For this design, I chose opaque glass for the subject and translucent glass for the sky. This also brings the bird forward while letting the sky recede. There's also a contrast between the small tesserae used for the background and the large tesserae used for the bird.

Materials
- Bird feeder with removable acrylic plastic panel
- Wood sealant
- Stained glass
- Clear contact paper
- Sticky mesh
- Clear silicone glue with caulk gun
- Cementitious grout
- Grout sealant

Tools
- Felt-tip marker
- Pistol-grip glass cutter
- Glass runner
- Two-wheeled nipper
- Painter's tape
- Matte board, 3 × 2-in. piece with a straight edge
- Dust mask
- Bucket
- Bowl
- Flat mixing trowel
- Rubber grout float
- Cotton cloths
- Small sponge

Template, page 270

To increase the lifespan of your bird feeder, use a wood sealant to protect the wood panels from the elements. When using sealant, work outdoors or in a well-ventilated room.

1. **Prepare the substrate.** The panel slides in and out of the bird feeder, so you need to leave enough space around the mosaic for the panel to fit back into the feeder. Before you remove the acrylic-plastic panel from the bird feeder, use a marker to draw an outline on the panel indicating the space that the mosaic will fit into. In addition, you'll need to leave a ⅛-in. border inside the outline for a shoulder that will be grouted later.

2. **Secure the cartoon and sticky mesh to the substrate.** After you've drawn the outline, remove the acrylic-plastic panel from the bird feeder and lay it flat on a worktable. Lay the cartoon face-up on the substrate and place sticky mesh—sticky side up—on top of the cartoon. If the sticky mesh inhibits your view of the design, use a marker to darken the lines of the cartoon. Then, tape down the corners with painter's tape to affix the cartoon and sticky mesh to the substrate so that your work surface and design will be secure and properly aligned while you lay the tiles. Double-check the cartoon and sticky mesh to make sure the design fits inside the outline you drew in step 1, and that there's a ⅛-in. border inside the outline for the shoulder.

3. **Dry lay the tesserae.** Dry lay the entire composition directly on the sticky mesh over the cartoon. When you get to the corners, remove the painter's tape so that the tesserae can properly adhere to the sticky mesh. Finalize the design at this stage and check the borders to ensure that no tesserae have crept over the edges of the cartoon. If they have, switch them out for smaller pieces to avoid creating a sharp edge or an insufficient shoulder for grouting.

4. **Cover the composition with contact paper.** Take a sheet of contact paper, slightly larger than the composition, and gently place it—sticky side down—on the surface of the mosaic, locking all the tesserae in place. Press the contact paper firmly onto each and

every tessera, being mindful of the sharp edges under the contact paper. Use a balled-up cloth to press the tesserae down, to avoid cutting yourself.

5. **Remove the composition from the substrate.** Before you can apply adhesive to the substrate, you must first remove the cartoon and sticky mesh from its surface. The easiest way to do this is with the aid of a flipper board—a board that you use to flip the composition over. The board can be any flat, lightweight board you have on hand—a spare piece of wood, plastic, or wedi board. As long as it's slightly larger than your mosaic, it will work.

    To safely remove your composition, place the flipper board on top of it. Hold both the top and bottom boards (the bottom being the substrate) securely—with the tesserae sandwiched safely in between—and simply flip them over. After you've executed the flip, your substrate will be on top of the pile. Remove it and face it right-side up on your work surface.

6. **Remove the cartoon and sticky mesh.** Remove the cartoon and gently pull the sticky mesh off the tesserae, being careful to pull slowly to avoid dislodging any tesserae from the contact paper underneath. Discard the sticky mesh.

7. **Apply silicone glue to the substrate.** Now that your substrate is bare, it's ready for adhesive. Follow the directions in Applying Silicone Glue on page 46. Apply the silicone glue to the side of the substrate that does not have the outline drawn on it, so that you can clean the ink off later. Use the outline as a guide to where you should apply silicone glue, cover the outlined area completely.

8. **Flip-and-set the composition back onto the substrate.** Follow the directions in step 7 of the Address Sign mosaic on page 80.

continued on page 89

I used large shapes where possible, since the substrate is so small. I like how the sticks of glass make pretty tail feathers, and the single yellow piece suggests the curve of the bird's breast.

I used *opus vermiculatum* for the design, outlining the bird with a single row of tesserae.

This design has lovely *andamento* in the background. The alignment of the tesserae suggests a breeze blowing past the bird. I enhanced the *andamento* with a line of darker glass at the bottom right.

Here's another example of a mosaicked bird feeder. I used a taller feeder and filled the frame with a bold cardinal on a leafy background.

9. **Seat the tesserae.** Smooth down the entire composition through the contact paper, pressing each tessera into the silicone glue to ensure adhesion. Use a balled-up cloth during this process to avoid cutting yourself on any sharp edges. Place an even weight (such as a book) on the top of the mosaic to help the setting process, and let the silicone glue begin to cure for approximately 30 minutes. After 30 minutes, gently lift a corner of the contact paper. If you feel confident that you can pull away the contact paper without pulling up any tesserae, do so. Pull slowly, pressing each tessera into the silicone. This is an important step to keep the grout from creeping under the tesserae later. If necessary, you can do any last fine-tuning to the mosaic design.

10. **Clean up any extra adhesive.** The adhesive will be visible in the interstices. This is a problem only if it has squished up between the tesserae so much that it might block the grout. It's sometimes difficult to see if silicone glue has squished up, because it dries clear. A good way to check for problem spots is to look at the contact paper after you pull it off—if it's spotted with silicone, the adhesive has risen above the level of the tesserae. If you see any problem spots, clean them out using a small painter's trowel or a thin piece of wire. Then let the silicone glue cure for 24 hours.

11. **Grout and polish the mosaic.** Follow the directions in Grouting Your Mosaic on page 49, but do not seal the mosaic just yet.

12. **Clean off the felt-tip marker outline and re-insert the acrylic plastic panel.** Once the grout has fully cured, clean off all traces of the felt-tip marker you used to outline the mosaic's border. Then, slide the acrylic plastic panel into the bird feeder.

13. **Seal the grout.** After 48 hours, apply grout sealant to the mosaic, following the directions in Grouting Your Mosaic.

continued from page 85

Watch out for grout creep! If a tessera is not completely seated into the silicone, it leaves a pocket where grout can creep in. When you hold your finished mosaic up to the light, you'll see the dark grout that has crept underneath the tesserae. Prevent grout creep by firmly pressing each and every tessera into the silicone.

This friendly raccoon peers out from a leafy backdrop.

Friendly Raccoon Face

EASY

To create this raccoon face, I used a very graphic design with strong value changes between the black and white tesserae. I made deliberate choices for the tesserae shapes—long, curved pieces for the whiskers, diamond and triangle pieces for the raccoon's fur; and angular shapes for the leaves in the background. This mosaic includes some objects—black marbles for the eyes and a stone for the nose. The three-dimensional pieces add modestly to the working time, since they have to be set by hand, but they make the face come alive.

For the substrate I used a cement pier block, which is available at hardware stores. Once the mosaic is finished, set the pier block on its side so that the raccoon face looks out onto the garden. Like the cement paver used for the Spiral Stepping-Stone mosaic, cement pier blocks are ready to be mosaicked—they don't need to be sealed. The pier block measures 12 × 12 in., but the working surface for the mosaic will be 10½ × 10½ in., so make your cartoon 10½ × 10½ in.

Materials

- 12 × 12-in. cement pier block
- Stained glass
- Two flat-back marbles (for the eyes)
- One smooth stone (for the nose)
- Sticky mesh
- Clear contact paper
- Thin-set mortar
- Cementitious grout
- Grout sealant

Tools

- Felt-tip marker
- Pistol-grip glass cutter
- Glass runner
- Two-wheeled nipper
- Painter's tape
- Dust mask
- Bucket
- Bowl
- Flat mixing trowel
- Notched metal trowel
- Rubber grout float
- Small painter's trowel
- Cotton cloths
- Small sponge

Template, page 271

1. **Secure the cartoon and sticky mesh to a temporary substrate.** Although this mosaic will ultimately end up on the pier block, it's much more convenient to work on a lightweight temporary substrate such as wood or wedi board. Keep in mind that your cartoon should be $10\frac{1}{2} \times 10\frac{1}{2}$ in. so that it will fit on the pier block with a border of at least $\frac{1}{8}$-in. between the edge of the cartoon and the edge of the pier block in order to leave enough space for a shoulder that will be grouted later. Lay the cartoon face-up on the temporary substrate and place sticky mesh—sticky side up—on top of the cartoon. If the sticky mesh inhibits your view of the design, use a marker to darken the lines of the cartoon. Then, tape down the corners with painter's tape to affix the cartoon and sticky mesh to the temporary substrate so that your work surface and design will be secure and properly aligned while you lay the tiles.

2. **Dry lay the tesserae.** Dry lay the entire composition, including the eyes and nose, directly on the sticky mesh over the cartoon. When you get to the corners, remove the painter's tape so that the tesserae can properly adhere to the sticky mesh. Finalize the design at this stage and check the borders to ensure that no tesserae have crept over the edges of the cartoon. If they have, switch them out for smaller pieces to avoid creating a sharp edge or an insufficient shoulder for grouting.

3. **Cover the composition with contact paper.** When you finish laying the tesserae, remove the three-dimensional objects (the marble eyes and the stone nose); they'll be set later. Take a sheet of contact paper, slightly larger than the composition, and gently place it—sticky side down—on the surface of the mosaic, locking all the tesserae in place. Press the contact paper firmly onto each and every tessera, being mindful of the sharp edges under the contact paper. To avoid cutting yourself, use a balled-up cloth to press the tesserae down.

4. **Remove the composition from the temporary substrate.** With the aid of a flipper board—a board that you use to flip the composition over—remove the composition from the temporary substrate. The board can be any flat, lightweight board you have on hand—a spare piece of wood, plastic, or wedi board. As long as it's slightly larger than your mosaic, it will work.

To safely remove your composition, place the flipper board on top of it. Hold both the top and bottom boards (the bottom being the temporary substrate) securely—with the tesserae sandwiched safely in between—and simply flip them over. After you've executed the flip, the temporary substrate will be on top of the pile.

Remove the temporary substrate. Gently pull the cartoon and sticky mesh away from the tiles, being careful to pull slowly to avoid dislodging the tiles from the contact paper underneath. Discard the sticky mesh.

5. **Apply thin-set mortar to the pier block.** Follow the directions in Preparing and Applying Thin-Set Mortar on page 42.

6. **Drape-and-set the composition onto the substrate.** When a substrate is too heavy to pick up comfortably, you can drape-and-set your composition onto it.

To begin, rotate the composition so that the top edge of the mosaic is closest to you. Using a balled-up cloth, give the composition another sweep over the contact paper. Then, firmly take hold of the corners of the contact paper that are closest to you. Lift the contact paper and, measuring with your eyes, align the composition with the substrate. Gently drape the composition onto the substrate, tile side down. The contact paper holds the tesserae better when you hold it so that it hangs vertically; try to avoid holding it horizontally. Once you've laid it down, you can shift it more precisely into place so that it's centered on the substrate. If any tesserae popped off the contact paper, fit them back into the design.

I've dry laid the composition on a temporary substrate, which is a more convenient working surface than the cement pier block. I originally drew the cartoon with pencil, but darkened the lines with a felt-tip marker for better visibility through the sticky mesh.

I used diamond and triangle shapes to suggest fur, and long curved pieces to suggest whiskers. The border is composed of a uniform set of tiles. Since there aren't any squares in the raccoon's face, the border tiles are a nice contrast.

The background consists of medium-tone greens. As you work, be sure to keep the color values separated—don't put a light-colored tessera directly next to one of the white tesserae used for the raccoon's face.

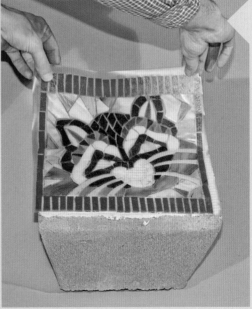

Here, I'm estimating the position of the mosaic before I drape it fully onto the pier block.

Once you've draped the mosaic onto the substrate, you can adjust the composition by gently tugging on the corners of the contact paper.

You can alter the raccoon design with any animal you choose. This mosaic is also on a pier block and features two birds made of fused glass.

7. **Seat the tesserae.** Smooth down the entire composition through the contact paper, pressing each tessera into the thin-set mortar to ensure adhesion. Use a balled-up cloth during this process to avoid cutting yourself on any sharp edges. Place an even weight (such as a book) on the top of the mosaic to help the setting process, and let the mortar begin to cure for approximately 30 minutes. After 30 minutes, gently lift a corner of the contact paper. If you feel confident that you can pull away the contact paper without pulling up any tesserae, do so. The mortar will still be wet at this point, so if necessary you can do some final fine-tuning to the mosaic design. After you've pulled off the contact paper, hand-set the three-dimensional pieces, adding a touch of existing thin-set mortar to the back of each.

8. **Clean up any extra adhesive.** The adhesive will be visible in the interstices. This is a problem only if it has squished up between the tesserae so much that it might block the grout. A good way to check for problem spots is to look at the contact paper after you pull it off—if it's spotted with mortar, the adhesive has risen above the level of the tesserae. If you see any problem spots, clean them out using a small painter's trowel or a thin piece of wire. Then let the thin-set mortar cure for 24 hours.

9. **Grout, polish, and seal the mosaic.** Follow the directions in Grouting Your Mosaic on page 49.

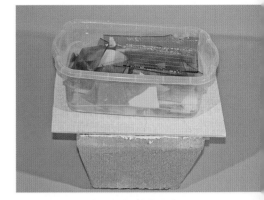

I've placed a board and a bin full of glass on the mosaic to weigh it down for 30 minutes.

Butter the backs of the marbles and the stone with thin-set mortar, and set them into place.

The bold contrasting colors of this simple spiral design have big visual impact.

Spiral Stepping-Stone

EASY

This stepping-stone mosaic is a beginner-level project that can have a big impact in your garden. The spiral design is simple and timeless, and the bold colors are eye-catching. Stepping-stones are fun to use for walkways in your garden, or just as neat pieces of color popping up at ground level wherever you choose to place them.

For this project, I used a 12 × 12-in. cement paver that I purchased at a hardware store. Precast cement pieces are ready to be mosaicked—they don't need sealing or any other preparation.

For the color scheme, I decided to use contrasting colors of blue and orange. Notice how the interior of the spiral is made up of darker orange tesserae, which creates depth, and then transitions outward to lighter orange tesserae. The transition gives the impression that the spiral is coming toward you—it's a neat trick of perception.

Materials

- 12 × 12-in. cement paver
- Cartoon
- Stained glass
- Sticky mesh
- Clear contact paper
- Thin-set mortar
- Cementitious grout
- Grout sealant

Tools

- Felt-tip marker
- Pistol-grip glass cutter
- Glass runner
- Two-wheeled nipper
- Painter's tape
- Dust mask
- Bucket
- Bowl
- Flat mixing trowel
- Notched metal trowel
- Small painter's trowel
- Rubber grout float
- Cotton cloths
- Small sponge

Template, page 272

1. **Secure the cartoon and sticky mesh to a temporary substrate.** Though this mosaic will ultimately end up on the cement paver, it's much more convenient to work on a lightweight 12 × 12-in. temporary substrate such as wood or wedi board. Your cartoon should fit on the 12 × 12-in. temporary substrate with a border of at least ⅛-in. between the edge of the cartoon and the edge of the substrate in order to leave enough space for a shoulder that will be grouted later. Lay the cartoon face-up on the temporary substrate and place sticky mesh—sticky side up—on top of the cartoon. If the sticky mesh inhibits your view of the design, use a marker to darken the lines of the cartoon. Then, tape down the corners with painter's tape to affix the cartoon and sticky mesh to the temporary substrate so that your work surface and design will be secure and properly aligned while you lay the tiles.

2. **Dry lay the tesserae.** Dry lay the entire composition directly on the sticky mesh over the cartoon. When you get to the corners, remove the painter's tape so that the tesserae can properly adhere to the sticky mesh. Finalize the design at this stage and check the borders to ensure that no tesserae have crept over the edges of the cartoon.

The sticky mesh and cartoon are taped to a temporary substrate, and I've begun to dry lay the tesserae. Notice the lines I've drawn on some of the tesserae using a felt-tip marker. I'll score and cut those pieces to create custom shapes.

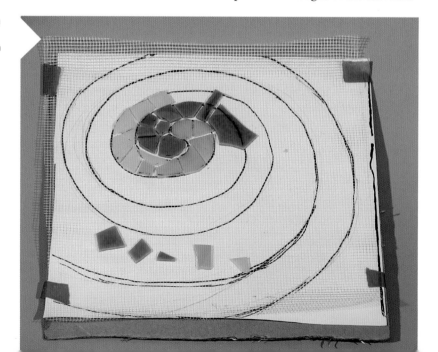

If they have, switch them out for smaller pieces to avoid creating a sharp edge or an insufficient shoulder for grouting.

3. **Cover the composition with contact paper.** Take a sheet of contact paper, slightly larger than the composition, and gently place it—sticky side down—on the surface of the mosaic, locking all the tesserae in place. Press the contact paper firmly onto each and every tessera, being mindful of the sharp edges under the contact paper. To avoid cutting yourself, use a balled-up cloth to press the tesserae down.

4. **Remove the composition from the temporary substrate.** With the aid of a flipper board—a board that you use to flip the composition over—remove the composition from the temporary substrate. The board can be any flat, lightweight board you have on hand—a spare piece of wood, plastic, or wedi board. As long as it's slightly larger than your mosaic, it will work.

   To safely remove your composition, place the flipper board on top of it. Hold both the top and bottom boards (the bottom being the temporary substrate) securely—with the tesserae sandwiched safely in between—and simply flip them over. After you've executed the flip, the temporary substrate will be on top of the pile.

   Remove the temporary substrate. Gently pull the cartoon and sticky mesh away from the tiles, being careful to pull slowly to avoid dislodging the tiles from the contact paper underneath. Discard the sticky mesh.

5. **Apply thin-set mortar to the cement paver.** Follow the directions in Preparing and Applying Thin-Set Mortar on page 42.

6. **Drape-and-set the composition onto the substrate.** When a substrate is too heavy to pick up comfortably, you can drape-and-set your composition onto it.

   To begin, rotate the composition so that the top edge of the mosaic is closest to you. Using a balled-up cloth, give the composition

As the spiral widened, I transitioned from using a single tessera per color field to two tesserae per color field. When you're filling in a color field, the outside edges need to form a smooth line. The interior edges (when you're using two tesserae per color field) can have some variation, but make sure the edges between colors are neat. You can even create a more deliberate grout line, possibly slightly thicker, to really highlight the separation of color fields.

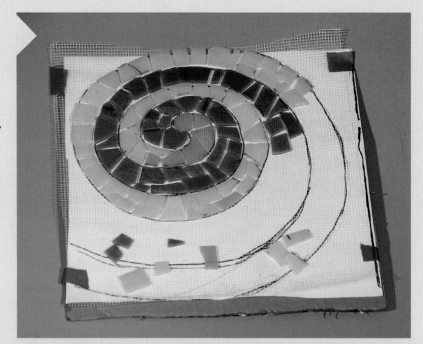

When you're coming toward the edge, be sure to leave room for the spiral to wind around, while still leaving a ⅛-in. shoulder for grout. Before you finish laying the tesserae, use a tape measure to double-check that your design will fit the dimensions of the cement paver.

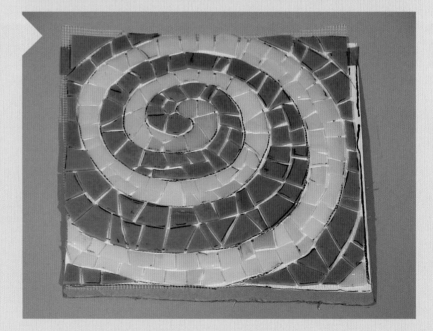

another sweep over the contact paper. Then, firmly take hold of the corners of the contact paper that are closest to you. Lift the contact paper, and, measuring with your eyes, align the composition with the substrate, and gently drape the composition onto the substrate, tile side down. The contact paper holds the tesserae better when you hold it so that it hangs vertically; try to avoid holding it horizontally. Once you've laid it down, you can shift it more precisely into place so that it's centered on the substrate. If any tesserae popped off the contact paper, fit them back into the design.

7. **Seat the tesserae.** Smooth down the entire composition through the contact paper, pressing each tessera into the thin-set mortar to ensure adhesion. Use a balled-up cloth during this process to avoid cutting yourself on any sharp edges. Place an even weight (such as a book) on the top of the mosaic to help the setting process, and let the mortar begin to cure for approximately 30 minutes. After 30 minutes, gently lift a corner of the contact paper. If you feel confident that you can pull away the contact paper without pulling up any tesserae, do so. The mortar will still be wet at this point, so if necessary you can do some final fine-tuning to the mosaic design.

8. **Clean up any extra adhesive.** The adhesive will be visible in the interstices. This is a problem only if it has squished up between the tesserae so much that it might block the grout. A good way to check for problem spots is to look at the contact paper after you pull it off—if it's spotted with mortar, the adhesive has risen above the level of the tesserae. If you see any problem spots, clean them out using a small painter's trowel or a thin piece of wire. Then let the thin-set mortar cure for 24 hours.

9. **Grout, polish, and seal the mosaic.** Follow the directions in Grouting Your Mosaic on page 49.

With mosaic fruits and veggies, your garden will bloom all year long.

Avocado

EASY

What could be more appropriate for a garden than fruits and veggies? This ripe avocado will keep your garden looking bountiful no matter the season. And you can use the techniques shown here to create mosaics of any of your harvest favorites—broccoli, strawberries, and more.

This mosaic is a good example of *opus musivum*. I began with the pit at the center, using different values of a cool brown to create a curved effect, and then worked outward from there, extending the curved effect to the borders, which gives a pleasing sense of flow to the piece.

1. **Secure the cartoon and sticky mesh to the substrate.** The cartoon should fit on the substrate, with a border of at least ⅛ in. between the edge of the cartoon and the edge of the substrate in order to leave enough space for a shoulder that will be grouted later. Lay the cartoon face-up on the prepared substrate and place sticky mesh—sticky side up—on top of the cartoon. If the sticky mesh inhibits your view of the design, use a marker to darken the lines of the cartoon. Then, tape down a few edges with painter's tape to affix the cartoon and sticky mesh to the substrate so that your work surface and design will be secure and properly aligned while you lay the tiles.

2. **Dry lay the tesserae.** Dry lay the entire composition directly on the sticky mesh over the cartoon. Concentric rows of tesserae in the

Materials

- Prepared wedi, cut from a 10 × 18-in. board (see Cutting Unique Shapes from Wedi Board), with hanger attached
- Gloves
- Fiberglass mesh tape
- Stained glass
- Sticky mesh
- Clear contact paper
- Thin-set mortar
- Cementitious grout
- Grout sealant

Tools

- Felt-tip marker
- Pistol-grip glass cutter
- Glass runner
- Two-wheeled nipper
- Utility knife
- Painter's tape
- Dust mask
- Bucket
- Bowl
- Flat mixing trowel
- Notched metal trowel
- Rubber grout float
- Small painter's trowel
- Cotton cloths
- Small sponge

Templates, pages 273, 274, 275

CUTTING UNIQUE SHAPES FROM WEDI BOARD

Wedi is an ideal substrate for curved shapes such as the one used in the Avocado, Dragonfly, and Hosta Leaf mosaics. Though we've already discussed the basic preparation for a wedi board substrate, irregular shapes are a bit more challenging. You still score and snap the wedi as usual, but with a bit more finesse and accuracy.

First, cut the curved avocado shape completely through the front side (the side you'll put the mosaic on) of the wedi. Then, make small relief cuts from the avocado shape out to the edges of the wedi so that you can eventually cut away sections one at a time to release the avocado. Finally, turn the wedi over—you'll see a visible perforation on the back side delineating the avocado. Use a utility knife to follow the perforation and cut completely through the cement coating.

Once you've cut the custom shape, prepare the edges of the wedi board as usual, wearing gloves to apply fiberglass mesh tape to the edges. Snip the tape at frequent intervals and layer it over itself so that it lies flat and doesn't bunch up around the curves. Apply thin-set mortar to the tape.

I brought out the contour of the pit by using different values of brown. The dark brown shows the base of the pit, the medium brown gives it the effect of projecting outward from the avocado flesh, and the lightest brown serves as a highlight on the top.

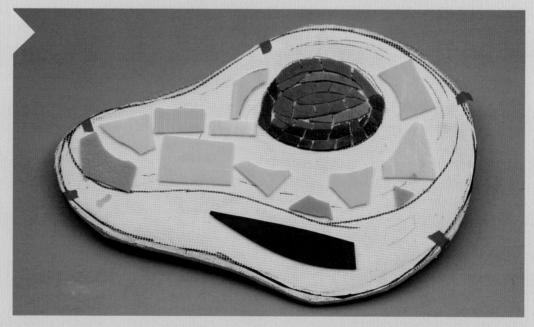

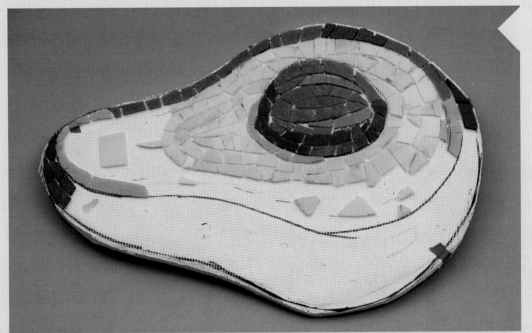

I used *opus musivum* to follow the curved shape of the avocado and create a rippled effect.

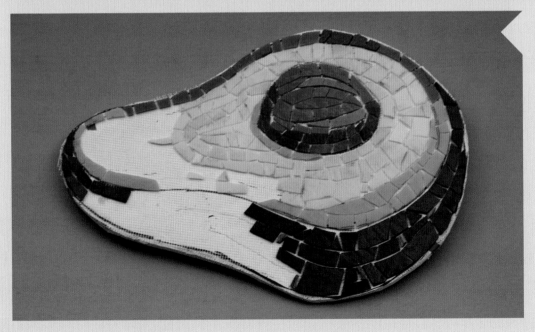

The dark skin contrasts well with the lighter flesh.

opus musivum style help to bring out the three-dimensional quality of the avocado. When you get to the edges, remove the painter's tape so that the tesserae can properly adhere to the sticky mesh. Finalize the design at this stage and check the borders to ensure that no tesserae have crept over the edges of the cartoon. If they have, switch them out for smaller pieces to avoid creating a sharp edge or an insufficient shoulder for grouting.

3. **Cover the composition with contact paper.** Take a sheet of contact paper, slightly larger than the composition, and gently place it—sticky side down—on the surface of the mosaic, locking all the tesserae in place. Press the contact paper firmly onto each and every tessera, being mindful of the sharp edges under the contact paper. To avoid cutting yourself, use a balled-up cloth to press the tesserae down.

4. **Remove the composition from the substrate.** Before you can apply adhesive to the substrate, you must first remove the cartoon and sticky mesh from its surface. The easiest way to do this is with the aid of a flipper board—a board that you use to flip the composition over. The board can be any flat, lightweight board you have on hand—a spare piece of wood, plastic, or wedi board. As long as it's slightly larger than your mosaic, it will work.

   To safely remove your composition, place the flipper board on top of it. Hold both the top and bottom boards (the bottom being the substrate) securely—with the tesserae sandwiched safely in between—and simply flip them over. After you've executed the flip, your substrate will be on top of the pile. Remove it and face it right-side up on your work surface.

5. **Remove the cartoon and sticky mesh.** Remove the cartoon and gently pull the sticky mesh off the tesserae, being careful to pull

slowly to avoid dislodging any tesserae from the contact paper underneath. Discard the sticky mesh.

6. **Apply thin-set mortar to the substrate.** Follow the directions in Preparing and Applying Thin-Set Mortar on page 42.

7. **Flip-and-set the composition back onto the substrate.** Follow the directions in step 7 of the Address Sign mosaic.

8. **Seat the tesserae.** Smooth down the entire composition through the contact paper, pressing each tessera into the thin-set mortar to ensure adhesion. Use a balled-up cloth during this process to avoid cutting yourself on any sharp edges. Place an even weight (such as a book) on the top of the mosaic to help the setting process, and let the mortar begin to cure for approximately 30 minutes. After 30 minutes, gently lift a corner of the contact paper. If you feel confident that you can pull away the contact paper without pulling up any tesserae, do so. The mortar will still be wet at this point, so if necessary you can do some final fine-tuning to the mosaic design.

9. **Clean up any extra adhesive.** The adhesive will be visible in the interstices. This is a problem only if it has squished up between the tesserae so much that it might block the grout. A good way to check for problem spots is to look at the contact paper after you pull it off—if it's spotted with mortar, the adhesive has risen above the level of the tesserae. If you see any problem spots, clean them out using a small painter's trowel or a thin piece of wire. Then let the thin-set mortar cure for 24 hours.

10. **Grout, polish, and seal the mosaic.** Follow the directions in Grouting Your Mosaic on page 49.

This oversize Hosta Leaf mosaic is a study in color, from deep greens to mellow yellows.

Hosta Leaf

MODERATE

Though this leaf design is simple, it gives you an opportunity to play with grout lines and color values. The more I looked at the hosta leaf—which I picked from my garden—the more color values I saw. If you want to show a significant progression of change in color value, use at least three or four values—a light, a dark, and a couple of mediums in between. This mosaic uses five different greens and three different yellows, and I added a red fused-glass ladybug for a spot of contrast.

This design also plays with grout lines in a deliberate way. I used narrow grout lines in the areas where I wanted to unify the colors, and then I used slightly wider grout lines at the points where I wanted to mimic the veins in the leaf. It's a subtle but effective way to use grout as an intentional element of the design. It creates the *andamento* of the leaf, which gives the work its continuity.

From light to dark, these are the color values used in this mosaic.

Materials

- Prepared wedi, cut from a 22 × 32-in. board (see Cutting Unique Shapes from Wedi Board, page 106), with hanger attached
- Fiberglass mesh tape
- Stained glass
- Ladybug or other three-dimensional object (optional)
- Sticky mesh
- Clear contact paper
- Thin-set mortar
- Cementitious grout
- Grout sealant

Tools

- Felt-tip marker
- Pistol-grip glass cutter
- Glass runner
- Two-wheeled nipper
- Painter's tape
- Dust mask
- Bucket
- Bowl
- Flat mixing trowel
- Notched metal trowel
- Rubber grout float
- Small painter's trowel
- Cotton cloths
- Small sponge
- Gloves

Template, page 276

1. **Draw your design on the substrate.** With a design as simple as this, you can draw your design directly onto the wedi board, but be sure to leave a border of 1/8 in. between the design and the edge of the substrate. (Though, of course, you can use a cartoon if you like. Sometimes it's hard to find a piece of paper this big.) Place sticky mesh—sticky side up—on top of the design. If the sticky mesh inhibits your view of the design, use a marker to darken the lines of the design. Then, tape down a few edges of the sticky mesh with painter's tape to secure it to the substrate so that the mesh will be secure and properly aligned with the design while you lay the tiles.

2. **Dry lay the tesserae.** Dry lay the entire composition directly on the sticky mesh. Finalize the design at this stage and check the borders to ensure that no tesserae have crept over the edges of the design. If they have, switch them out for smaller pieces to avoid creating a sharp edge or an insufficient shoulder for grouting.

3. **Cover the composition with contact paper.** If you used a three-dimensional object in your composition, such as the ladybug used in this mosaic, then you will need to remove it in order for the contact paper to firmly hold all the tesserae. Take a sheet of contact paper, slightly larger than the composition, and gently place it—sticky side down—on the surface of the mosaic, locking all the tesserae in place. Press the contact paper firmly onto each and every tessera, being mindful of the sharp edges under the contact paper. To avoid cutting yourself, use a balled-up cloth to press the tesserae down.

Using the drawing of the hosta leaf as a reference, I drew the design directly on the surface of the wedi and then placed the sticky mesh over it.

Here you can see the progression from yellow to green. I'll remove the fused-glass ladybug before I cover the mosaic with contact paper.

4. **Remove the composition from the substrate.** Lay a flipper board on top of the composition. Because of the unusual shape of this substrate, you might find it helpful to get the help of a friend or use a couple of woodworking clamps to hold the boards together securely. Hold both the top and bottom boards securely—your flipper board and your substrate, with the tesserae sandwiched safely in between—and flip them over. Set the substrate aside.

5. **Remove the sticky mesh.** Gently pull the sticky mesh off the tesserae, being careful to pull slowly to avoid dislodging any tesserae from the contact paper underneath. Discard the sticky mesh.

6. **Apply thin-set mortar to the substrate.** Follow the directions in Preparing and Applying Thin-Set Mortar on page 42.

7. **Flip-and-set the composition back onto the substrate.** Follow the directions in step 7 of the Address Sign mosaic.

8. **Seat the tesserae.** Smooth down the entire composition through the contact paper, pressing each tessera into the thin-set mortar to ensure adhesion. Use a balled-up cloth during this process to avoid cutting yourself on any sharp edges. Place an even weight (such as a book) on the top of the mosaic to help the setting process, and let the mortar begin to cure for approximately 30 minutes. After 30 minutes, gently lift a corner of the contact paper. If you feel confident that you can pull away the contact paper without pulling up any tesserae, do so. The mortar will still be wet at this point, so if necessary you can do some final fine-tuning to the mosaic design.

   Hand-set any three-dimensional objects, such as the ladybug, adding a touch of thin-set mortar to the back of each.

9. **Clean up any extra adhesive.** The adhesive will be visible in the interstices. This is a problem only if it has squished up between the tesserae so much that it might block the grout. A good way to check for problem spots is to look at the contact paper after you pull it off—if it's spotted with mortar, the adhesive has risen above the level of the tesserae. If you see any problem spots, clean them out using a small painter's trowel or a thin piece of wire. Then let the thin-set mortar cure for 24 hours.

10. **Grout, polish, and seal the mosaic.** Follow the directions in Grouting Your Mosaic on page 49.

I used slightly exaggerated grout lines to show the veins of the leaf. This photograph also shows the three different colors used in the stem—they help differentiate the bottom of the stem from the top.

Take a deep breath and let your eyes "walk" around and around the path toward the center of this meditative labyrinth.

Labyrinth

EASY

Since ancient times, people have walked labyrinths as a form of meditation. Now, you can bring that peaceful respite to your garden with this labyrinth mosaic.

The most challenging aspect of this mosaic is the actual design—figuring out the measurements for both the tesserae and the grout spacing in between. Luckily, I've done that for you! The template provided is designed to fit a 22 × 22-in. substrate, using precut ¾ in. ceramic tesserae. As you seat the labyrinth tiles, you can use it as a time of reflection. It's exciting to learn the circuitous path, which has a metaphorical implication about getting to the center of things.

I used a very simple palette of white and brown tiles. Neutral tones emphasize the meditative quality of the piece, and the simplicity of the one color for the entire labyrinth keeps the viewer's focus on the design of the entire labyrinth, rather than on the individual tiles. I find that using lighter tiles for the labyrinth and darker ones for the border adds to the idea of looking inward.

Grouting plays an integral role in the design. The white tesserae are the pathway of the labyrinth, while the grout lines form the walls that separate the pathway. To emphasize this distinction, I used slightly wider grout lines, slightly thicker than ⅛ in., to denote the walls. As for grout color, a dark grout unifies the background and lets it recede, giving prominence to the labyrinth itself.

Materials
- Prepared wedi or cement backer board, 22 × 22 in., with hanger attached
- Ceramic tile or vitreous glass, precut ¾ in. (approximately 325 light tiles for the path and 250 dark tiles for the border)
- Sticky mesh
- Clear contact paper
- Thin-set mortar
- Cementitious grout
- Grout sealant

Tools
- Ceramic tile nipper (if you're using ceramic tiles)
- Felt-tip marker
- Pistol-grip glass cutter
- Glass runner
- Two-wheeled nipper
- Painter's tape
- Dust mask
- Bucket
- Bowl
- Flat mixing trowel
- Notched metal trowel
- Rubber grout float
- Small painter's trowel
- Cotton cloths
- Small sponge

Template, page 277

The how-to directions provided here are for a 22 × 22-in. mosaic. I highly recommend scaling up the template to those dimensions. If you'd like to use a smaller substrate, scale up the template to 14⅝ × 14⅝ in. and use ⅝-in. tiles. If you opt to make a mosaic of a different size, your results will, of course, vary.

1. **Secure the cartoon and sticky mesh to the substrate.** Your cartoon should fit on the substrate, with a border of at least ⅛-in. between the edge of the cartoon and the edge of the substrate in order to leave enough space for a shoulder that will be grouted later. Lay the cartoon face-up on the prepared substrate and place sticky mesh—sticky side up—on top of the cartoon. If the sticky mesh inhibits your view of the design, use a marker to darken the lines of the cartoon. Then, tape down the corners with painter's tape to affix the cartoon and sticky mesh to the substrate so that your work surface and design will be secure and properly aligned while you lay the tiles.

2. **Dry lay the tesserae.** Dry lay the entire composition directly on the sticky mesh over the cartoon. If you'd like, start with the first tile of the path—it's interesting to build the labyrinth by following it. Pay extra attention to the spacing of the tesserae from one curve to the next. Notice how half a tile is used to fill in the grout line when the path makes a 180° turn. Notice as well how you need to use trapezoid- and triangle-shaped tiles to make the turns on the small, inner circles, but you can use full tiles for the entire outer circle. When you get to the corners, remove the painter's tape so that the tesserae can properly adhere to the sticky mesh. Finalize the design at this stage and check the borders to ensure that no tesserae have crept over the edges of the cartoon. If they have, switch them out for smaller pieces to avoid creating a sharp edge or an insufficient shoulder for grouting.

Notice the precision of the grout lines.

Tapered pieces will help you make the tight turns of the labyrinth's inner circles.

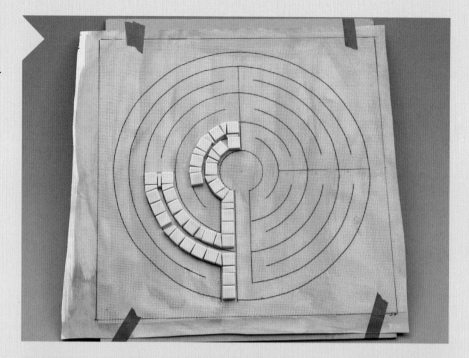

Once you get to the outer rings of the labyrinth, the work will go much more quickly because you can make the turns using full tiles.

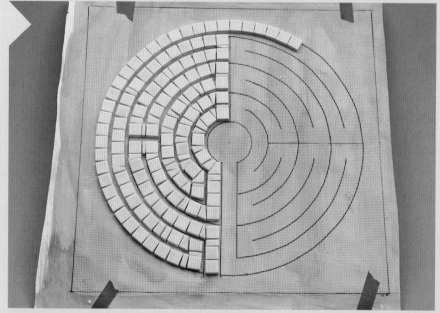

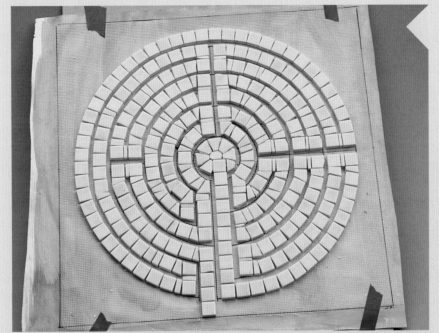

For the center of the labyrinth, I formed a circle using tesserae shaped like trapezoids. To make the tesserae at the center of the circle, I used a two-wheeled nipper to nibble the edges of a ceramic tile. Make sure the lead stone—the one that starts the path at the bottom of the mosaic—reaches the edge of the substrate, to give the labyrinth a starting point.

The background is a great example of *opus regulatum*. When you're tiling the background, work from the corners, using whole pieces as much as you can. To surround the edges of the circle, use triangle shapes, which you can cut using a two-wheeled nipper.

If you're using predominantly white tesserae, and your cartoon is on white paper, brush a light wash of thinned tempera or acrylic paint—in a color that contrasts well with your tiles—on the cartoon to create a contrast between the paper and the tesserae.

3. **Cover the composition with contact paper.** Take a sheet of contact paper, slightly larger than the composition, and gently place it—sticky side down—on the surface of the mosaic, locking all the tesserae in place. Press the contact paper firmly onto each and every tessera, being mindful of the sharp edges under the contact paper. To avoid cutting yourself, use a balled-up cloth to press the tesserae down.

4. **Remove the composition from the substrate.** Before you can apply adhesive to the substrate, you must first remove the cartoon and sticky mesh from its surface. The easiest way to do this is with the aid of a flipper board—a board that you use to flip the composition over. The board can be any flat, lightweight board you have on hand—a spare piece of wood, plastic, or wedi board. As long as it's slightly larger than your mosaic, it will work.

   To safely remove your composition, place the flipper board on top of it. If your board feels too big to turn over, get the help of a friend or use a couple of spring clamps to hold the boards together securely. Hold both the top and bottom boards (the bottom being the substrate) securely—with the tesserae sandwiched safely in between—and simply flip them over. After you've executed the flip, your substrate will be on top of the pile. Remove it and face it right-side up on your work surface.

5. **Remove the cartoon and sticky mesh.** Remove the cartoon and gently pull the sticky mesh off the tesserae, being careful to pull slowly to avoid dislodging any tesserae from the contact paper underneath. Discard the sticky mesh.

6. **Apply thin-set mortar to the substrate.** Follow the directions in Preparing and Applying Thin-Set Mortar on page 42.

7. **Flip-and-set the composition back onto the substrate.** Follow the directions in step 7 of the Address Sign mosaic. Make sure the hanger is properly aligned in relation to the mosaic before you set the substrate on the composition.

8. **Seat the tesserae.** Smooth down the entire composition through the contact paper, pressing each tessera into the thin-set mortar to ensure adhesion. Use a balled-up cloth during this process to avoid cutting yourself on any sharp edges. Place an even weight (such as a book) on the top of the mosaic to help the setting process, and let the mortar begin to cure for approximately 30 minutes. After 30 minutes, gently lift a corner of the contact paper. If you feel confident that you can pull away the contact paper without pulling up any tesserae, do so. The mortar will still be wet at this point, so if necessary you can do some final fine-tuning to the mosaic design.

9. **Clean up any extra adhesive.** The adhesive will be visible in the interstices. This is a problem only if it has squished up between the tesserae so much that it might block the grout. A good way to check for problem spots is to look at the contact paper after you pull it off—if it's spotted with mortar, the adhesive has risen above the level of the tesserae. If you see any problem spots, clean them out using a small painter's trowel or a thin piece of wire. Then let the thin-set mortar cure for 24 hours.

10. **Grout, polish, and seal the mosaic.** Follow the directions in Grouting Your Mosaic on page 49.

An old window sash gets a second life with this glass-on-glass mosaic. Notice how opaque glass gives a sense of solidity to the bamboo stalks, while the translucent glass in the background suggests the light, airy sky.

Bamboo Stand on Recycled Window

MODERATE

The Bamboo Stand on Recycled Window is a good example of *opus sectile*—large pieces surrounded by smaller tesserae.

This project is a great opportunity to hone your skills in cutting custom tesserae. The tesserae in the bamboo stand have a lot of repetition in them, so it makes sense to cut them all at once. The design calls for approximately thirty leaves—fifteen smaller leaves and fifteen bigger leaves. I cut the leaves assembly-line style, starting with 3-in. rectangles in two values of opaque green glass and cutting them using the technique described in Cutting Gently Curved Shapes on page 28.

To create the stalks, I cut about twenty rectangular sticks and then rounded their edges using a nipper. For contrast, I chose brown stained glass for the nodes on the stalks and for the skinny offshoots.

I wanted to fill the background with two values of blue transparent glass, but I didn't need any custom shapes, so I created a bank of blue glass tesserae to use to fill the background.

For this mosaic, a background of transparent glass usually works best. Old windows are readily available at home reuse centers. It's fun to make something new out of something old, and a window sash makes an excellent built-in frame. When you're working with glass-on-glass, there's always a delightful surprise when you first see how the finished piece looks with sunlight shining through it.

Materials

- Recycled window, approximately 24 in. long (including the frame), prepared as described in Working with and Hanging a Recycled Window below
- Stained glass
- Sticky mesh
- Clear contact paper
- Clear silicone glue with caulk gun
- Cementitious grout
- Grout sealant

Tools

- Felt-tip marker
- Pistol-grip glass cutter
- Glass runner
- Two-wheeled nipper
- Painter's tape
- Matte board, 3×2-in. piece with a straight edge
- Spring clamps
- Additional boards for flipping (wedi board or pieces of cardboard)
- Dust mask
- Bucket
- Bowl
- Flat mixing trowel
- Rubber grout float
- Cotton cloths
- Small sponge

Template, page 278

WORKING WITH AND HANGING A RECYCLED WINDOW

A recycled window makes an excellent substrate, but keep in mind that your mosaic will be large. House windows are typically pretty big. Keep an eye out for a smaller window—ideally 24 inches on the longest side. Don't be seduced by a big one—you'll be in for a lot more work!

To prepare the window, sand down the frame as needed to remove any peeling paint or splintered wood. Clean the glass with window cleaner and chip away any spots of paint on the glass so that they don't interfere with the mosaic. Don't worry about streaks and scratches—they'll be covered by the mosaic.

To hang a window sash, pre-drill two holes at the top corner and insert $12 \times 1\frac{1}{8}$-in. eye screws. Loop covered wire between the two screws, creating a triangle. Be sure to allow for appropriate hanging length for the location. Depending on where you plan to hang the mosaic, you may have to tie it down at the bottom as well as the top, to prevent it from swaying in the wind.

1. **Place the cartoon and sticky mesh onto the substrate.** Lay your cartoon face-up on the prepared substrate, making sure that the cartoon fits neatly within the dimensions of the window sash. Place sticky mesh—sticky side up—on top of the cartoon. If the sticky mesh inhibits your view of the design, use a marker to darken the lines of the cartoon. Then, tape down the corners with painter's tape to affix the cartoon and sticky mesh to the substrate so that your work surface and design will be secure and properly aligned while you lay the tiles.

2. **Dry lay the tesserae.** Dry lay the entire composition directly on the sticky mesh over the cartoon. Begin the bamboo areas by laying in the large leaf and stem pieces first. Decide on the shape, size, and direction of the tesserae to create a sense of *andamento*. When you get to the corners, remove the painter's tape so that the tesserae can properly adhere to the sticky mesh. Finalize the design at this stage.

3. **Cover the composition with contact paper.** Take a sheet of contact paper, slightly larger than the composition, and gently place it—sticky side down—on the surface of the mosaic, locking all the tesserae in place. Make sure the contact paper is not touching the inside edge of the window frame. Press the contact paper firmly onto each and every tessera, being mindful of the sharp edges under the contact paper. To avoid cutting yourself, use a balled-up cloth to press the tesserae down.

4. **Remove the composition from the substrate.** Before you can apply adhesive to the substrate, you must first remove the cartoon and sticky mesh from its surface. The easiest way to do this is with the aid of a flipper board—a board that you use to flip the composition over. The board can be any flat, lightweight board you have on hand—a spare piece of wood, plastic, or wedi board. As long as it's slightly larger than your mosaic, it will work.

Use rectangular-shaped sticks for the bamboo stems. You can add a slight curve to the lengths or nip off the corners of the rectangles to give them a natural look.

For the background, I used a dark blue transparent tesserae, with some lighter tesserae mixed in. The background tesserae are mostly squares, but there is some variety of shapes in areas where it was necessary to get in between the leaves.

I added a spiral to make a focal point on the left side. The color of the left side is reversed from that of the right side to create a visually interesting transition across the piece. I didn't plan for it during my initial design, but it was a happy result of experimenting as I went along. The spiral implies how bamboo grows and grows.

above To keep the composition from moving when you turn it over, fill up the window recess with a couple pieces of cardboard, and then lay your flip board over the top.

right You can also use clamps to hold everything together for extra security as you turn the window frame over.

For this project, the flipper board should fit inside the window frame. However, if the board is larger than the window frame, you'll need to place a few pieces of cardboard in the recess between the composition and the board to prevent the composition from moving when you flip it. Hold both the top and bottom boards (the bottom being the substrate) securely—with the tesserae and cardboard sandwiched safely in between—and simply flip them over. After you've executed the flip, your substrate will be on top of the pile. Remove it and face it right-side up on your work surface. Leave the composition on the flipper board and pieces of cardboard, because you'll eventually put the window back on the composition, and you'll need the board and cardboard in order for the window frame to fit around the composition.

5. **Remove the cartoon and sticky mesh.** Remove the cartoon and gently pull the sticky mesh off the tesserae, being careful to pull slowly to avoid dislodging any tesserae from the contact paper underneath. Discard the sticky mesh.

6. **Apply silicone glue to the substrate.** Follow the directions in Applying Silicone Glue on page 46.

7. **Flip-and-set the composition back onto the substrate.** Follow the directions in step 7 of the Address Sign mosaic, remembering to use extra cardboard layers with the flipper board.

8. **Seat the tesserae.** Smooth down the entire composition through the contact paper, pressing each tessera into the silicone glue to ensure adhesion. Use a balled-up cloth during this process to avoid cutting yourself on any sharp edges. Place an even weight (such as a book) on the top of the mosaic to help the setting process, and let the silicone glue begin to cure for approximately 30 minutes. After 30 minutes, gently lift a corner of the contact paper. If you feel confident that you can pull away the contact paper without pulling up any tesserae, do so. The glue will still be wet at this point, so if necessary you can do some final fine-tuning to the mosaic design. Pull slowly, pressing each tessera into the silicone. This is an important step to keep the grout from creeping under the tesserae later.

9. **Clean up any extra adhesive.** The adhesive will be visible in the interstices. This is a problem only if it has squished up between the tesserae so much that it might block the grout. It's sometimes difficult to see if silicone glue has squished up, because it dries clear. A good way to check for problem spots is to look at the contact paper after you pull it off—if it's spotted with silicone, the adhesive has risen above the level of the tesserae. If you see any problem spots, clean them out using a small painter's trowel or a thin piece of wire. Then let the silicone glue cure for 24 hours.

10. **Grout, polish, and seal the mosaic.** Follow the directions in Grouting Your Mosaic on page 49.

If you don't have a chicken coop, this mosaic is the next best thing. Notice how tall the chicken stands amidst the riot of straw and fresh eggs.

Chicken Coop

MODERATE

Materials
- Prepared wedi or cement backer board, 14 × 20 in., with hanger attached
- Cartoon
- Fiberglass mesh tape
- Stained glass
- Sticky mesh
- Clear contact paper
- Thin-set mortar
- Cementitious grout
- Grout sealant

Tools
- Felt-tip marker
- Pistol-grip glass cutter
- Glass runner
- Two-wheeled nipper
- Painter's tape
- Dust mask
- Bucket
- Bowl
- Flat mixing trowel
- Notched metal trowel
- Rubber grout float
- Small painter's trowel
- Cotton cloths
- Small sponge
- Gloves

Template, page 279

This mosaic was inspired by the city of Portland, Oregon, where it's not uncommon to walk around and see urban chicken coops. If you're not quite up to the task of actually raising your own chickens, this Chicken Coop mosaic is the next best thing.

Though the composition is fairly simple—a chicken, her eggs, and a coop—it also expresses the busyness of a chicken yard. The challenge with this mosaic is to differentiate the dark hen from the straw in the background. It's important to create visual separation between the elements and to show the chaos of the straw bed without making the overall composition overwhelming to the eye. I did this by using dark color values for the chicken and primarily lighter color values for the straw. Use a variety of sizes, shapes, colors, and values to make the hen stand out from the straw.

1. **Secure the cartoon and sticky mesh to the substrate.** Your cartoon should fit on the substrate, with a border of at least ⅛-in. between the edge of the cartoon and the edge of the substrate in order to leave enough space for a shoulder that will be grouted later. Lay the cartoon face-up on the prepared substrate and place sticky mesh—sticky side up—on top of the cartoon. If the sticky mesh inhibits your view of the design, use a marker to darken the lines of the cartoon. Then, tape down the corners with painter's tape to affix the cartoon and sticky mesh to the substrate so that

For the chicken, I used a combination of big and small pieces. The larger, dark-brown tesserae form the contour of the chicken and create a visual separation from the straw. The smaller tesserae in the interior give the impression of feathers.

The curves of the eggs create a contrast with the straight straw pieces. The difference between the light straw and the dark chicken is another strong contrast, which lets the chicken come forward.

This piece of glass is a darker value of blue. I used it for the sky because it lets the sky recede into the background, which gives a sense of distance and makes the foreground pop.

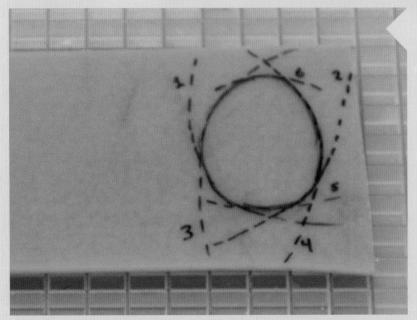

Cutting an ovoid shape is a challenge, but it's a must-have for the egg shapes in this mosaic. Use a felt-tip marker to draw an ovoid shape on a piece of stained glass. Then, using a pistol-grip glass cutter, cut four scores around the outline, making sure that the scores overlap each other. Using the cutter, score the entire dotted line. When all the lines have been scored, use the runner to split away all the extra glass, which leaves you with the egg shape. Sand down any sharp corners.

A millefiori gives life to the chicken's eye.

your work surface and design will be secure and properly aligned while you lay the tiles.

2. **Dry lay the tesserae.** Dry lay the entire composition directly on the sticky mesh over the cartoon. When you get to the corners, remove the painter's tape so that the tesserae can properly adhere to the sticky mesh. Finalize the design at this stage and check the borders to ensure that no tesserae have crept over the edges of the cartoon. If they have, switch them out for smaller pieces to avoid creating a sharp edge or an insufficient shoulder for grouting.

3. **Cover the composition with contact paper.** Take a sheet of contact paper, slightly larger than the composition, and gently place it—sticky side down—on the surface of the mosaic, locking all the tesserae in place. Press the contact paper firmly onto each and every tessera, being mindful of the sharp edges under the contact paper. To avoid cutting yourself, use a balled-up cloth to press the tesserae down.

4. **Remove the composition from the substrate.** Before you can apply adhesive to the substrate, you must first remove the cartoon and sticky mesh from its surface. The easiest way to do this is with the aid of a flipper board—a board that you use to flip the composition over. The board can be any flat, lightweight board you have on hand—a spare piece of wood, plastic, or wedi board. As long as it's slightly larger than your mosaic, it will work.

   To safely remove your composition, place the flipper board on top of it. Hold both the top and bottom boards (the bottom being the substrate) securely—with the tesserae sandwiched safely in between—and simply flip them over. After you've executed the flip, your substrate will be on top of the pile. Remove it and face it right-side up on your work surface.

5. **Remove the cartoon and sticky mesh.** Remove the cartoon and gently pull the sticky mesh off the tesserae, being careful to pull slowly to avoid dislodging any tesserae from the contact paper underneath. Discard the sticky mesh.

6. **Apply thin-set mortar to the substrate.** Follow the directions in Preparing and Applying Thin-Set Mortar on page 42.

7. **Flip-and-set the composition back onto the substrate.** Follow the directions in step 7 of the Address Sign mosaic.

8. **Seat the tesserae.** Smooth down the entire composition through the contact paper, pressing each tessera into the thin-set mortar to ensure adhesion. Use a balled-up cloth during this process to avoid cutting yourself on any sharp edges. Place an even weight (such as a book) on the top of the mosaic to help the setting process, and let the mortar begin to cure for approximately 30 minutes. After 30 minutes, gently lift a corner of the contact paper. If you feel confident that you can pull away the contact paper without pulling up any tesserae, do so. The mortar will still be wet at this point, so if necessary you can do some final fine-tuning to the mosaic design.

9. **Clean up any extra adhesive.** The adhesive will be visible in the interstices. This is a problem only if it has squished up between the tesserae so much that it might block the grout. A good way to check for problem spots is to look at the contact paper after you pull it off—if it's spotted with mortar, the adhesive has risen above the level of the tesserae. If you see any problem spots, clean them out using a small painter's trowel or a thin piece of wire. Then let the thin-set mortar cure for 24 hours.

10. **Grout, polish, and seal the mosaic.** Follow the directions in Grouting Your Mosaic on page 49.

This end table blends the modern and the rustic with its stark graphic design and recycled wooden legs.

Flower Tabletop

EASY

Materials

- Cement backer board
- Chair, with backrest removed
- Cartoon
- Stained glass
- Sticky mesh
- Clear contact paper
- Thin-set mortar
- Urethane grout
- Approximately 74 in. length of ½-in. molding (for the frame on the back of the mosaic)
- Construction glue

Tools

- Felt-tip marker
- Pistol-grip glass cutter
- Glass runner
- Two-wheeled nipper
- Painter's tape
- Dust mask
- Bucket
- Bowl
- Flat mixing trowel
- Notched metal trowel
- Rubber grout float
- Small painter's trowel
- Cotton cloths
- Small sponge

Template, page 280

This sweet end table is an excellent way to reuse an old chair that has seen better days. Just cut away the backrest, and voilà—you now have table legs. Be sure that your substrate is large enough to fit comfortably over the seat. This seat is 18 × 18 in., so I used a 20 × 20-in. substrate for the mosaic.

To create this design, I cut a flower-shaped stencil from a piece of paper and simply stenciled it on to the cartoon in different places, reversing it and varying the size so that the design wouldn't look like wallpaper. I liked the vertical nature of the design, as it mimics the upward growth of flowers, so I put a border on only the long sides to enhance the sense of length. When you're creating flowers, use two different color values to show depth. Placing the darker tiles toward the bottom of the flower adds a sense of volume. Tapered cuts work well as petals.

For mosaic tabletops, I highly recommend using cement backer board because of its durability and weather resistance.

I cut off the backrest to turn an old chair into table legs.

1. **Secure the cartoon and sticky mesh to the substrate.** Your cartoon should fit on the substrate, with a border of at least $1/8$-in. between the edge of the cartoon and the edge of the substrate in order to leave enough space for a shoulder that will be grouted later. Lay the cartoon face-up on the prepared substrate and place sticky mesh—sticky side up—on top of the cartoon. If the sticky mesh inhibits your view of the design, use a marker to darken the lines of the cartoon. Then, tape down the corners with painter's tape to affix the cartoon and sticky mesh to the substrate so that your work surface and design will be secure and properly aligned while you lay the tiles. (You can also place long tiles around the edge of the sticky mesh, instead of tape, to hold everything in place, as I did.)

2. **Dry lay the tesserae.** Dry lay the entire composition directly on the sticky mesh over the cartoon. When you get to the corners, remove the painter's tape so that the tesserae can properly adhere to the sticky mesh. Finalize the design at this stage and check the borders to ensure that no tesserae have crept over the edges of the cartoon. If they have, switch them out for smaller pieces to avoid creating a sharp edge or an insufficient shoulder for grouting.

3. **Cover the composition with contact paper.** Take a sheet of contact paper, slightly larger than the composition, and gently place it—sticky side down—on the surface of the mosaic, locking all the tesserae in place. Press the contact paper firmly onto each and every tessera, being mindful of the sharp edges under the contact paper. To avoid cutting yourself, use a balled-up cloth to press the tesserae down.

4. **Remove the composition from the substrate.** Before you can apply adhesive to the substrate, you must first remove the cartoon and sticky mesh from its surface. The easiest way to do this is with

Here you can see the simple stenciled cartoon I used as the basis for this design. Mosaic pieces will make each flower unique.

The mosaic's white background provides a strong contrast with the subject matter. I used larger tapered cuts for the background to echo the tapered pieces used for the red flower petals.

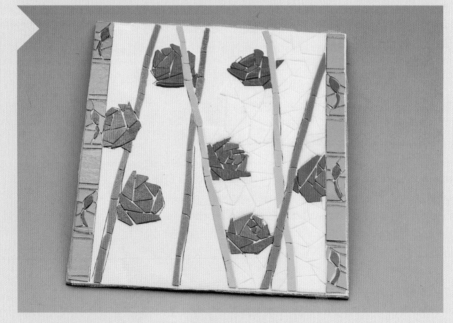

The flowers are somewhat self-contained, while there's more variety and action in the background. This effect will be enhanced by the gray grout.

When you're making a tabletop mosaic, consider mosaicking the edges, as seen in this example. Mosaicked edges add strength to the piece, and they're aesthetically pleasing. If you want to mosaic the edges, do it after all of the tesserae have been set.

the aid of a flipper board—a board that you use to flip the composition over. The board can be any flat, lightweight board you have on hand—a spare piece of wood, plastic, or wedi board. As long as it's slightly larger than your mosaic, it will work.

To safely remove your composition, place the flipper board on top of it. Hold both the top and bottom boards (the bottom being the substrate) securely—with the tesserae sandwiched safely in between—and simply flip them over. After you've executed the flip, your substrate will be on top of the pile. Remove it and face it right-side up on your work surface.

5. **Remove the cartoon and sticky mesh.** Remove the cartoon and gently pull the sticky mesh off the tesserae, being careful to pull slowly to avoid dislodging any tesserae from the contact paper underneath. Discard the sticky mesh.

6. **Apply thin-set mortar to the substrate.** Follow the directions in Preparing and Applying Thin-Set Mortar on page 42.

7. **Flip-and-set the composition back onto the substrate.** Follow the directions in step 7 of the Address Sign mosaic.

8. **Seat the tesserae.** Smooth down the entire composition through the contact paper, pressing each tessera into the thin-set mortar to ensure adhesion. Use a balled-up cloth during this process to avoid cutting yourself on any sharp edges. Place an even weight (such as a book) on the top of the mosaic to help the setting process, and let the mortar begin to cure for approximately 30 minutes. After 30 minutes, gently lift a corner of the contact paper. If you feel confident that you can pull away the contact paper without pulling up any tesserae, do so. The mortar will still be wet at this point, so if necessary you can do some final fine-tuning to the mosaic design.

9. **Clean up any extra adhesive.** The adhesive will be visible in the interstices. This is a problem only if it has squished up between the tesserae so much that it might block the grout. A good way to check for problem spots is to look at the contact paper after you pull it off—if it's spotted with mortar, the adhesive has risen above the level of the tesserae. If you see any problem spots, clean them out using a small painter's trowel or a thin piece of wire. Then let the thin-set mortar cure for 24 hours.

10. **Grout the mosaic with urethane grout.** Urethane has a built-in adhesive to make it stronger, but it tends to dry fast and is harder to clean, so it's best to grout and clean one section of the mosaic at a time, in less than 15 minutes each. Grout an area that is approximately 10 × 10 in., then stop grouting and use a damp sponge to clean the grouted area. Scrub repeatedly in a circular motion to get the excess grout off the mosaic surface. (You need to use more elbow grease when you're working with urethane grout.) After you've cleaned the area, proceed with the next section of the mosaic. When you're grouting a mosaic tabletop, be extra careful to protect the edges. You don't want to use too much grout on the edges—use enough grout to give it an approximately ⅛-in. coat. Any more than this would create a bump that would be more susceptible to breaking away.

11. **Place the mosaic on the chair.** To secure the finished mosaic snugly to the chair, attach a frame that will fit around the chair and to the back side of the mosaic. Be sure that the inside dimensions of the frame are slightly larger than the chair so that the frame fits over the chair. To make the frame, use construction adhesive to glue four pieces of ½-in. wood molding to the back side of the mosaic.

Because of their greater exposure to moisture, dirt, and fallen leaves, horizontal outdoor mosaics call for urethane grout. Although it's more challenging to work with urethane grout than cementitious grout—urethane dries faster and is harder to clean—urethane grout is stronger.

Gather with friends (or alone with a good book!) around this inviting table.

Round Tabletop

CHALLENGING

Elements of this mosaic were inspired by the Buddhist mandala—a circular design that represents many elements of the natural world. The design seems particularly apt for a garden environment, as the circle represents growth from the center, radiating outward.

This project calls for a tempered-glass tabletop, which you can find (along with a base) at a home decor store. Tempered glass is stronger than conventional window glass, and it doesn't break easily, so it's ideal for a patio table.

Because the size of the mosaic makes it difficult to flip-and-set, I used two working methods for this project: the direct method for the border and double-direct-with-slide method for the interior.

1. **Lay the border of the mosaic using the direct method.** When you're working with a repeated border pattern that stretches out over a large area, the direct method is most effective for laying glass tesserae. Determine the design for the border beforehand and follow it through around the tabletop. You can do a quick dry lay of the border, or even just a section of the border, to see whether you like the pattern before you commit to adhering it. Then remove the tesserae.

A leafy vine gently wraps around the contours of the tabletop.

Materials

- Tempered glass tabletop (36-in. diameter, 3/8-in. thick) and base
- Cartoon
- Stained glass
- Sticky mesh
- Clear contact paper
- Silicone glue with caulk gun
- Urethane grout

Tools

- Felt-tip marker
- Pistol-grip glass cutter
- Glass runner
- Two-wheeled nipper
- Sanding block
- Painter's tape
- Dust mask
- Bucket
- Bowl
- Flat mixing trowel
- Notched metal trowel
- Rubber grout float
- Small painter's trowel
- Cotton cloths
- Small sponge
- 12 × 12-in. board (for sliding the mosaic onto the substrate)
- 3 or 4 pieces of 3 × 2-in. matte board with a straight edge

Template for the inner circle, page 281

2. **Prepare a bank of tesserae.** When you're working in the direct method, it's important to have enough tesserae on hand so that you can seat them before the silicone glue dries. Cut a bank of tesserae for the border. Use the sanding block to sand the outside edges of the tesserae that will be on the outermost edge of the table so that they won't cut anyone.

3. **Dry lay a segment of the border.** Dry lay one repeat of the border design, or approximately 8 inches of the border. Take a similar-sized piece of contact paper and gently place it—sticky side down—on the surface of the tesserae, locking them in place. Press the contact paper firmly onto each and every tessera, being mindful of the sharp edges under the contact paper. Use a balled-up cloth to press the tesserae down, to avoid cutting yourself. Draw an outline on the substrate around the area the tesserae will cover so that you can see the area in which to apply silicone glue. Lift the contact paper, with the border tesserae attached, and set them aside.

4. **Apply silicone glue.** Apply a squiggle of silicone glue to the outlined area on the tempered glass. Use a small piece of matte board to smooth the silicone evenly across the area to be mosaicked.

5. **Seat the tesserae.** Place a small dot of silicone glue on each tessera and seat it firmly into the silicone glue on the table. If excess glue rises above the surface level of the tesserae, clean it out with a small painter's trowel or pencil.

6. **Repeat steps 3, 4, and 5 for the rest of the border.** As you work, you can figure out how many full repeats you'll need.

7. **Lay the interior ring using the double-direct-with-slide method.** Follow the directions in Double-Direct-with-Slide.

The border of the table is a simple geometric pattern based on parallelograms. You can see where I've applied a squiggle of silicone glue for the area to be mosaicked next.

A lazy Susan is helpful to have for a large round project like this one—it lets you easily rotate the piece while you work.

The flower design at the center of the mosaic was inspired by a flower arrangement. I was stumped as to what to put in the center, and stumbled upon an arrangement when I was out getting a coffee. The inspiration you can find when you keep your eyes open is amazing.

8. **Lay the inner circle using double-direct-with-slide.** If the tempered glass has a hole in the center, cut a piece of glass with a diameter larger than the hole and use silicone glue to attach it to the underside of the table covering the hole. Then layer a few pieces of circular glass inside the hole to shim it up and create a surface for your mosaic to adhere to. Make sure that the center tessera is large enough to cover the shimmed-up area; it will help disguise the hole. Once you've seated the entire mosaic, let the silicone glue cure for 24 hours.

9. **Grout the mosaic with urethane grout.** Urethane has a built-in adhesive to make it stronger, but it tends to dry fast and is harder to clean, so it's best to grout and clean one section of the mosaic at a time, in less than 15 minutes each. Grout an area that is approximately 10 × 10 in., then stop grouting and use a damp sponge to clean the grouted area. Scrub repeatedly in a circular motion to get the excess grout off the mosaic surface. (You need to use more elbow grease when you're working with urethane grout.) After you've cleaned the area, proceed with the next section of the mosaic. Grout will not hold to the sides of a glass substrate. When you reach the edges of the table, just smooth the grout into the shoulder. This will secure the outermost tesserae.

DOUBLE-DIRECT-WITH-SLIDE

This method resembles the double-direct method, but with two major differences. First, instead of flipping or draping your composition into place, you slide it into place using a board. Second, rather than dry laying the entire composition at one time, you dry lay it in small segments and adhere the segments one at a time.

This method is especially good for two-dimensional mosaics larger than four square feet. When you work on a large mosaic, you have to be creative!

Use a board to slide the mosaic segment into place.

1. **Secure the cartoon and sticky mesh to one segment of the substrate.** Lay the cartoon face-up on the substrate and place sticky mesh—sticky side up—on top of the cartoon. (If you're working with a glass substrate, another option is to place the cartoon underneath the glass, as I did with this project.) Remember that you're only going to work on one segment at a time, so only set out about one square foot of sticky mesh, or enough to cover the segment you're working on. If the sticky mesh inhibits your view of the design, use a marker to darken the lines of the cartoon. Then, tape down the edges with painter's tape to affix the cartoon and sticky mesh to the substrate so that your work surface and design will be secure and properly aligned while you lay the tiles.

2. **Dry lay the segment.** Dry lay the segment of the composition you're working on directly on the sticky mesh over the cartoon. For the best results, leave a 1-in. buffer zone between segments untiled, and set those areas directly once all the segments are in place. This will help you create a smooth transition between segments. When you reach the taped edges, remove the painter's tape so that the tesserae can properly adhere to the sticky mesh. Finalize the design of the segment at this stage. If you're working near the edge of the substrate, check the composition to ensure that no tesserae have crept over the edges of the cartoon. If they have, switch them out for smaller pieces to avoid creating a sharp edge or an insufficient shoulder for grouting.

Cover the composed segment with contact paper. Take a sheet of clear contact paper, slightly larger than the composed segment, and gently place it—sticky side down—on the surface of the segment, locking all the tesserae in place. Press the contact paper firmly onto each and every tessera, being mindful of the sharp edges under the contact paper. To avoid cutting yourself, use a balled-up cloth to press the tesserae down. Use a felt-tip marker to draw an outline around the segment, so that you can see the area you'll need to apply silicone glue to.

3. **Lift the segment from the substrate.** Grasp the corners of the contact paper, lift the segment, and place it upside down on a slider board. Remove the cartoon and carefully pull off the sticky mesh. Lift the segment again, turn it over, and place it back on the board with the contact paper–side up. Unlike the typical double-direct method, the mosaic is now right-side up, ready to slide onto the substrate.

4. **Apply the adhesive to the substrate.** Working on the area you outlined, apply the adhesive (thin-set mortar or silicone glue, whichever adhesive the project calls for) to the substrate. Follow the directions in Preparing and Applying Thin-Set Mortar on page 42 or Applying Silicone Glue on page 46.

5. **Slide-and-set the composed segment back onto the substrate.** Carefully pick up the slider board and grab a corner of the contact paper. Measuring with your eyes, line up the composed segment with its corresponding area on the substrate. Slide the mosaic directly onto the substrate by touching down one corner and then slowly pulling the board out from under the composition.

6. **Repeat the process for each remaining area of the mosaic.** Set each segment of the mosaic following the steps above until you've finished seating the tesserae.

7. **Fill in the buffer zones between segments using the direct method.**

It's always a delight to catch sight of a dragonfly flitting through the garden, its wings shimmering in the sunlight.

Dragonfly

EASY

This mosaic is a stylized graphic design of an oversize dragonfly flitting across a flowered background. I chose to work with small rectangles to create *andamento*, or flow, in the wings and the background. To suggest the shimmering translucence of the wings, I used a variety of stained glass, marbles, and millefiori. You can have a lot of fun playing with color in this mosaic. I chose a dark grout to provide contrast with the lightness of the translucent glass in the wings, as if the grout lines were the exaggerated veins of the wings themselves.

1. **Secure the cartoon and sticky mesh to the substrate.** Your cartoon should fit on the substrate, with a border of at least ⅛ in. between the edge of the cartoon and the edge of the substrate in order to leave enough space for a shoulder that will be grouted later. Lay the cartoon face-up on the prepared substrate and place sticky mesh—sticky side up—on top of the cartoon. If the sticky mesh inhibits your view of the design, use a marker to darken the lines of the cartoon. Then, tape down a few edges with painter's tape to affix the cartoon and sticky mesh to the substrate so that your work surface and design will be secure and properly aligned while you lay the tiles.

2. **Dry lay the tesserae.** Dry lay the entire composition directly on the sticky mesh over the cartoon. When you get to the edges, remove the painter's tape so that the tesserae can properly adhere to the

Materials
- Prepared wedi, cut from a 15 × 20-in. board (see Cutting Unique Shapes from Wedi Board, page 106), with hanger attached
- Fiberglass mesh tape
- Stained glass
- Flat-back marbles
- Millefiori
- Sticky mesh
- Clear contact paper
- Thin-set mortar
- Cementitious grout
- Grout sealant

Tools
- Felt-tip marker
- Two-wheeled nippers
- Glass runner
- Painter's tape
- Dust mask
- Bucket
- Bowl
- Flat mixing trowel
- Notched metal trowel
- Rubber grout float
- Small painter's trowel
- Cotton cloths
- Small sponge
- Gloves

Template, page 282

Translucent glass conveys the light, shimmering quality of the dragonfly's wings.

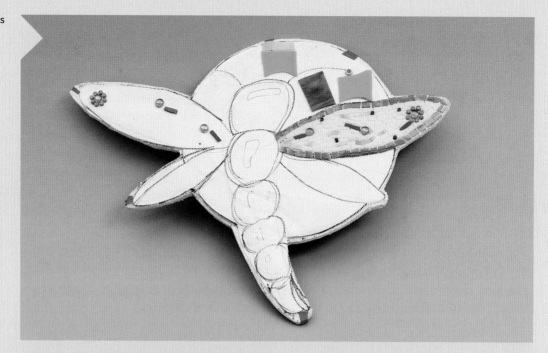

The opaque body supplies a strong contrast to the translucent wings. I used *opus sectile*—large circles cut from dark glass—to show the segments of the body.

Warm colors in the background contrast with the cool colors of the dragonfly. There's no need to create a complex design; you want the background to both unite with and separate from the dragonfly. It's a busy piece, so you need some color contrast to visually separate the dragonfly from its background.

Millefiori and marbles provide eye-catching accents to the dragonfly's wings.

sticky mesh. Finalize the design at this stage and check the borders to ensure that no tesserae have crept over the edges of the cartoon. If they have, switch them out for smaller pieces to avoid creating a sharp edge or an insufficient shoulder for grouting.

3. **Cover the composition with contact paper.** First, pull out the marbles and millefiori pieces so they don't interfere with the contact paper. Take a sheet of contact paper, slightly larger than the composition, and gently place it—sticky side down—on the surface of the mosaic, locking all the tesserae in place. Press the contact paper firmly onto each and every tessera, being mindful of the sharp edges under the contact paper. To avoid cutting yourself, use a balled-up cloth to press the tesserae down.

4. **Remove the composition from the substrate.** Before you can apply adhesive to the substrate, you must first remove the cartoon and sticky mesh from its surface. The easiest way to do this is with the aid of a flipper board—a board that you use to flip the composition over. The board can be any flat, lightweight board you have on hand—a spare piece of wood, plastic, or wedi board. As long as it's slightly larger than your mosaic, it will work.

    To safely remove your composition, place the flipper board on top of it. Hold both the top and bottom boards (the bottom being the substrate) securely—with the tesserae sandwiched safely in between—and simply flip them over. After you've executed the flip, your substrate will be on top of the pile. Remove it and face it right-side up on your work surface.

5. **Remove the cartoon and sticky mesh.** Remove the cartoon and gently pull the sticky mesh off the tesserae, being careful to pull slowly to avoid dislodging any tesserae from the contact paper underneath. Discard the sticky mesh.

6. **Apply thin-set mortar to the substrate.** Follow the directions in Preparing and Applying Thin-Set Mortar on page 42. When you're working with unusually shaped substrates, such as this dragonfly, be sure to apply adhesive in all the corners of the substrate.

7. **Flip-and-set the composition back onto the substrate.** Follow the directions in step 7 of the Address Sign mosaic. Since this shape is so unusual, it is easier to lay the substrate in the correct position.

8. **Seat the tesserae.** Smooth down the entire composition through the contact paper, pressing each tessera into the thin-set mortar to ensure adhesion. Use a balled-up cloth during this process to avoid cutting yourself on any sharp edges. Place an even weight (such as a book) on the top of the mosaic to help the setting process, and let the mortar begin to cure for approximately 30 minutes. After 30 minutes, gently lift a corner of the contact paper. If you feel confident that you can pull away the contact paper without pulling up any tesserae, do so. The mortar will still be wet at this point, so if necessary you can do some final fine-tuning to the mosaic design. Hand-set the marbles and millefiori now, adding a touch of existing thin-set mortar to the back of each.

9. **Clean up any extra adhesive.** The adhesive will be visible in the interstices. This is a problem only if it has squished up between the tesserae so much that it might block the grout. A good way to check for problem spots is to look at the contact paper after you pull it off—if it's spotted with mortar, the adhesive has risen above the level of the tesserae. If you see any problem spots, clean them out using a small painter's trowel or a thin piece of wire. Then let the thin-set mortar cure for 24 hours.

10. **Grout, polish, and seal the mosaic.** Follow the directions in Grouting Your Mosaic on page 49.

If you don't live
near the ocean,
you can bring the
ocean to you.

Flowing Wave

MODERATE

Materials

- Prepared wedi, cut from a 16 × 36-in. board (see Cutting Unique Shapes from Wedi Board, page 106), with hanger attached
- Fiberglass mesh tape
- Stained glass
- Strings of beads (optional)
- Sticky mesh
- Clear contact paper
- Thin-set mortar
- Cementitious grout
- Grout sealant

Tools

- Felt-tip marker
- Pistol-grip glass cutter
- Glass runner
- Two-wheeled nipper
- Painter's tape
- Dust mask
- Bucket
- Bowl
- Flat mixing trowel
- Notched metal trowel
- Rubber grout float
- Small painter's trowel
- Cotton cloths
- Small sponge
- Gloves

No matter how landlocked you are, this Flowing Wave mosaic will bring the ocean into your garden. This project is an ideal opportunity to practice creating *andamento*, because the placement of your tesserae conveys the flow and eddy of the water. For colors, use white and light blue tesserae at the top to suggest the crest of the wave, and use darker colors at the bottom to convey the ocean's depth. A dark grout gives unity to the darker areas while highlighting the choppy, foamy nature of the ocean in the lighter areas.

1. **Secure the cartoon and sticky mesh to the substrate.** Your cartoon should fit on the substrate, with a border of at least ⅛-in. between the edge of the cartoon and the edge of the substrate in order to leave enough space for a shoulder that will be grouted later. Lay the cartoon face-up on the prepared substrate and place sticky mesh—sticky side up—on top of the cartoon. If the sticky mesh inhibits your view of the design, use a marker to darken the lines of the cartoon. Then, tape down a few edges with painter's tape to affix the cartoon and sticky mesh to the substrate so that your work surface and design will be secure and properly aligned while you lay the tiles.

Template, page 283

Notice how the dark blue tesserae in the center create a sense of flow in the piece, conveying the idea of water swelling upward into a wave.

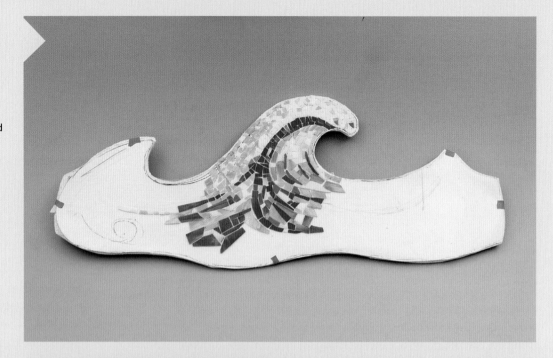

The smaller pieces at the top of the wave suggest frothy water, whereas the larger pieces below show the depth and enormity of the ocean. *Andamento* is created in this mosaic by giving more emphasis to the horizontal grout lines than the vertical.

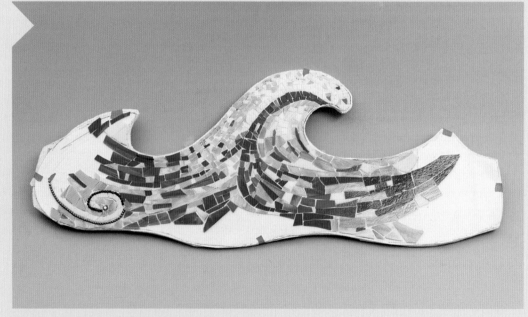

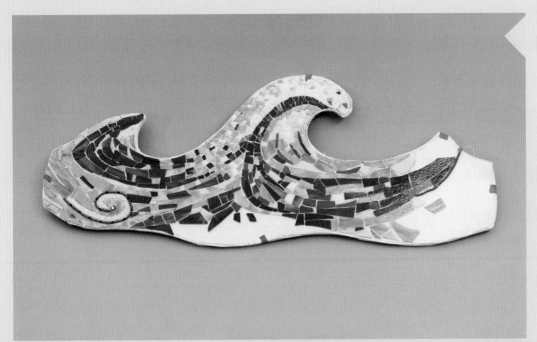

Strings of beads help suggest that the water is eddying and swirling.

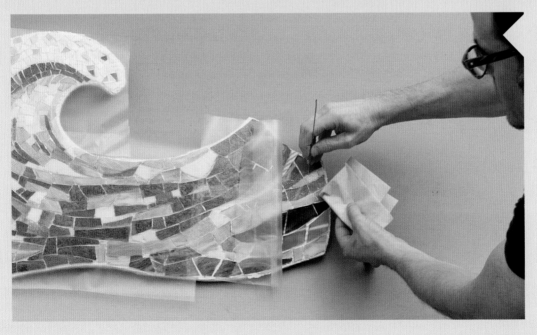

I'm cleaning off excess adhesive that has squished up between the tesserae.

2. **Dry lay the tesserae.** Dry lay the entire composition directly on the sticky mesh over the cartoon. When you get to the edges, remove the painter's tape so that the tesserae can properly adhere to the sticky mesh. Finalize the design at this stage and check the borders to ensure that no tesserae have crept over the edges of the cartoon. If they have, switch them out for smaller pieces to avoid creating a sharp edge or an insufficient shoulder for grouting.

3. **Cover the composition with contact paper.** First, remove the strings of beads (if you used them) so that they don't interfere with the contact paper. Take a sheet of contact paper and gently place it—sticky side down—onto a portion of the surface of the mosaic, locking all the tesserae in place. With a substrate this large, you'll need to use several sheets of contact paper. Press the contact paper firmly onto each and every tessera, being mindful of the sharp edges under the contact paper. To avoid cutting yourself, use a balled-up cloth to press the tesserae down. Repeat this process for the other portions of the mosaic.

4. **Remove the composition from the substrate.** Before you can apply adhesive to the substrate, you must first remove the cartoon and sticky mesh from its surface. The easiest way to do this is with the aid of a flipper board—a board that you use to flip the composition over. The board can be any flat, lightweight board you have on hand—a spare piece of wood, plastic, or wedi board. As long as it's slightly larger than your mosaic, it will work.

   To safely remove your composition, place the flipper board on top of it. If your board feels too big to turn over, get the help of a friend or use a couple of spring clamps to hold the boards together securely. Hold both the top and bottom boards (the bottom being the substrate) securely—with the tesserae sandwiched safely in between—and simply flip them over. After you've executed the flip, your substrate will be on top of the pile. Remove it and face it right-side up on your work surface.

5. **Remove the cartoon and sticky mesh.** Remove the cartoon and gently pull the sticky mesh off the tesserae, being careful to pull slowly to avoid dislodging any tesserae from the contact paper underneath. Discard the sticky mesh.

6. **Apply thin-set mortar to the substrate.** Follow the directions in Preparing and Applying Thin-Set Mortar on page 42. When you're working with unusually shaped substrates, such as this wave, be sure to apply adhesive in all the corners of the substrate.

7. **Flip-and-set the composition back onto the substrate.** Follow the directions in step 7 of the Address Sign mosaic. Since this shape is so unusual, it is easier to lay the substrate in the correct position.

8. **Seat the tesserae.** Smooth down the entire composition through the contact paper, pressing each tessera into the thin-set mortar to ensure adhesion. Use a balled-up cloth during this process to avoid cutting yourself on any sharp edges. Place an even weight (such as a book) on the top of the mosaic to help the setting process, and let the mortar begin to cure for approximately 30 minutes. After 30 minutes, gently lift a corner of the contact paper. If you feel confident that you can pull away the contact paper without pulling up any tesserae, do so. The mortar will still be wet at this point, so if necessary you can do some final fine-tuning to the mosaic design. Hand-set the strings of beads back into the mosaic.

9. **Clean up any extra adhesive.** The adhesive will be visible in the interstices. This is a problem only if it has squished up between the tesserae so much that it might block the grout. A good way to check for problem spots is to look at the contact paper after you pull it off—if it's spotted with mortar, the adhesive has risen above the level of the tesserae. If you see any problem spots, clean them out using a small painter's trowel or a thin piece of wire. Then let the thin-set mortar cure for 24 hours.

10. **Grout, polish, and seal the mosaic.** Follow the directions in Grouting Your Mosaic on page 49.

This whimsical mosaic and plant box can be displayed indoors or outdoors.

Tulip Mosaic with Plant Box

MODERATE

The plant box in this project brings the garden and the mosaic together. You can even display this one indoors to enjoy a touch of nature inside.

    This project consists of a three-dimensional object—a small wooden box—on a rigid two-dimensional substrate. Seating the tesserae around the box presented a bit of a challenge, so I used a combination of three different methods: direct, double-direct, and double-direct-with-slide.

    The design of the mosaic is simple—tulip buds in the foreground and rolling hills in the background. The blue border creates a pretty counterpart to the wooden box.

1. **Construct the planter box.** Follow the directions in How to Make a Wooden Box.

2. **Attach the box to the substrate.** Leaving enough room for the bottom border of the mosaic, secure the wooden box to the substrate using four 1-in. screws, placing two at the top corners of the box and two near the lower corners.

3. **Secure the cartoon and sticky mesh to the top half of the substrate.** For this project, you'll lay the composition in segments.

Materials

- Cement backer board, 14 × 22 in., with hanger attached
- Stained glass
- Sticky mesh
- Clear contact paper
- Wooden box, small enough to fit onto the substrate
- 1-in. screws
- Thin-set mortar
- Cementitious grout
- Grout sealant

Tools

- Screwdriver or drill
- Felt-tip marker
- Pistol-grip glass cutter
- Glass runner
- Two-wheeled nipper
- Painter's tape
- 12 × 12 board (for sliding the mosaic onto the substrate)
- Dust mask
- Bucket
- Bowl
- Flat mixing trowel
- Notched metal trowel
- Small painter's trowel
- Rubber grout float
- Small painter's trowel
- Cotton cloths
- Small sponge

Template, page 284

I made the little box out of recycled wood. If you have a box on hand that you want to use, go for it. Otherwise, it's easy to make one yourself.

Because it's so big, it's easier to mosaic this piece in four segments: top, sides, and bottom.

Create the cartoon and cut it into three pieces: one for the top half of the mosaic and one each for the lower left and right corners. (You'll set the area underneath the box directly, so you don't need to make a cartoon for it.) Place the cartoon pieces on the substrate, and use a felt-tip marker to draw an outline around each piece on the substrate. Each piece of the cartoon should fit on the substrate, with a border of at least ⅛-in. between the edge of the cartoon and the edge of the substrate in order to leave enough space for a shoulder that will be grouted later. Remove the pieces for the lower corners. Lay the cartoon for the top half of the mosaic face-up on the substrate and place sticky mesh—sticky side up—on top of the cartoon. If the sticky mesh inhibits your view of the design, use a marker to darken the lines of the cartoon. Then, tape down the corners with painter's tape to affix the cartoon and sticky mesh to the substrate so that your work surface and design will be secure and properly aligned while you lay the tiles.

4. **Dry lay the tesserae for the top half of the mosaic.** Dry lay the top half of the composition directly on the sticky mesh over the cartoon. When you get to the corners, remove the painter's tape so that the tesserae can properly adhere to the sticky mesh. Finalize the design at this stage and check the borders to ensure that no tesserae have crept over the edges of the cartoon. If they have, switch them out for smaller pieces to avoid creating a sharp edge or an insufficient shoulder for grouting. For the best results, leave a one-inch buffer zone between segments untiled, and set those areas directly once all the segments are in place. This helps create a smooth transition between segments.

5. **Cover the composition with contact paper.** Take a sheet of contact paper, slightly larger than the composition, and gently place it—sticky side down—on the surface of the mosaic, locking all the tesserae in place. Press the contact paper firmly onto each and

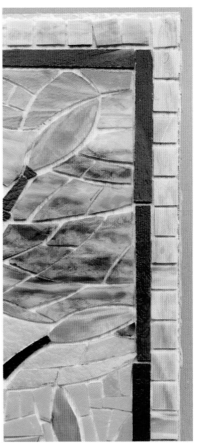

Light and dark green hues create contrast and depth in the design. The border is laid in *opus regulatum.*

every tessera, being mindful of the sharp edges under the contact paper. To avoid cutting yourself, use a balled-up cloth to press the tesserae down. Then, pick it up carefully by the corners of the contact paper and lay it upside-down on a board or work surface. Gently peel away the cartoon and sticky mesh. Apply thin-set mortar to the substrate—but only to the area you will set immediately (stay within the area you marked in step 3). Follow the directions in Preparing and Applying Thin-set Mortar on page 42.

6. **Drape-and-set the segment onto the substrate.** To begin, rotate the composition so that the top edge of the mosaic is closest to you. Using a balled-up cloth, give the composition another sweep across the contact paper. Then, firmly take hold of the corners of the contact paper that are closest to you. Lift the contact paper, and, measuring with your eyes, align the composition with the substrate, and gently drape the composition onto the substrate. The contact paper holds the tesserae better when you hold it so that it hangs vertically; try to avoid holding it horizontally. Once you've laid it down, you can shift it more precisely into place. If any tesserae popped off the contact paper, fit them back into the design. Smooth down the composition, again using a balled-up cloth, and be sure to press each tessera firmly into the thin-set mortar.

7. **Remove the contact paper.** Let the mortar cure for approximately 30 minutes. After 30 minutes, gently lift a corner of the contact paper. If you feel confident that you can pull away the contact paper without pulling up any tesserae, do so. The mortar will still be wet at this point, so if necessary you can do some final fine-tuning to the mosaic design.

8. **Clean up any extra adhesive.** The adhesive will be visible in the interstices. This is only a problem if it has squished up between the tesserae so much that it might block the grout. A good way to check for problem spots is to look at the contact paper after you pull it off—if it's spotted with mortar, the adhesive has risen above the level of the tesserae. If you see any problem spots, clean them out using a small painter's trowel or a thin piece of wire.

9. **Seat the left and right bottom sides using the double-direct-with-slide.** For the side pieces, dry lay the mosaic as described in steps 4 and 5. Then, take a sheet of contact paper, slightly larger than the segment, and gently place it—sticky side down—on the surface of the segment, locking all the tesserae in place. Press the contact paper firmly onto each and every tessera, being mindful of the sharp edges under the contact paper. To avoid cutting yourself, use a balled-up cloth to press the tesserae down. Pick it up carefully by the corners of the contact paper and lay it upside-down on a slider board. Gently peel away the cartoon and sticky mesh. Now flip the segment right-side up to prepare it for setting. Apply thin-set mortar to the substrate—but only to the area you will set immediately (stay within the area you marked in step 3).

10. **Slide-and-set the composed segments back onto the substrate.** Instead of draping the segments into place, you'll use the slide technique. Carefully pick up the slider board and grab a corner of the contact paper. Measuring with your eye, line up the composed segment with its corresponding area of the substrate. Slide the mosaic directly onto the substrate by touching down one corner and then slowly pulling out the board from under the composition.

11. **Remove the contact paper.** Follow the directions in step 7.

12. **Clean up any extra adhesive.** Follow the directions in step 8.

Here's a before-and-after scene. In the first photograph, you can see I've pulled away the bottom right corner segment, laid it aside, and applied thin-set to the substrate. In the next photograph, I'm using the slider board to gently slide the segment into place. In the third photograph, I repeat the process on the other side.

HOW TO MAKE A WOODEN BOX

It's fairly easy to make a small wooden planter to attach to a mosaic.

Materials
- Wooden board (1 × 6 × 30 in.)
- Finishing nails (1¼ in.)
- Sandpaper

Tools
- Wood glue
- Hammer
- Saw

Cut the 1 × 6 wood into five pieces with the following dimensions: base (5½ × 5½ in.); back (6 × 5½ in.); front (6½ × 2½ in.); and two sides (6 × 2¾ in.). Sand the edges. Add a bead of wood glue to each surface before nailing them together in order to make the structure stronger. Using two finishing nails per edge, nail the back piece to the base. Then nail the side pieces to the base and back. Finally, nail the front piece to the base and sides.

This exploded view shows where to insert the nails.

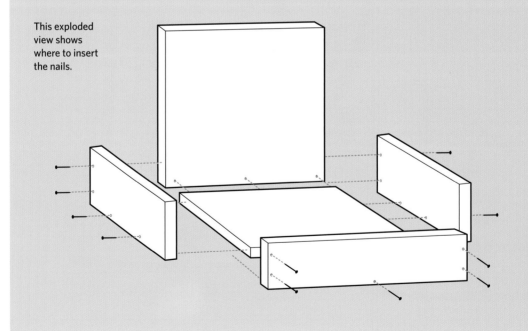

13. **Use the direct method to fill in the bottom part of the mosaic.** This final segment is small enough to fill in easily using the direct method. Use a small painter's trowel to apply a layer of thin-set mortar to the area, and seat the tesserae. Let the thin-set mortar cure for 24 hours.

14. **Grout, polish, and seal the mosaic.** Follow the directions in Grouting Your Mosaic on page 49, but before beginning the grouting process, tape off the wooden box to prevent getting grout on it. Simply cover the exposed edges of wood with painter's tape, and then grout the surrounding mosaic.

White grout shows grime, so it's usually not recommended for outdoor mosaics. But I couldn't resist in this case, because the white adds such a welcome brightness to this mosaic. You can help keep the grout white by periodically cleaning it with a solution of vinegar and water.

With this Found Objects mosaic, you can celebrate the cycles of nature and have fun working with three-dimensional inclusions.

Found Objects

MODERATE

An upcycled ceramic pitcher makes a perfect watering can.

Incorporating three-dimensional elements and found objects into a mosaic is a lot of fun. In this case, the gears add symbolism, implying that nature is a machine that works underground, churning out plants. This seems especially true in the Pacific Northwest, where I live, since plants grow so well here. And stones, of course, are in every garden.

For this mosaic, it's important to use ceramic tesserae. Ceramic is thicker than glass, and that thickness results in a stronger structural relationship between the tiles and the three-dimensional pieces. If the thickness of the found objects and the conventional tesserae differs too greatly, it can be difficult to make them work well together. Ceramic tiles force you to keep the design simple, because they are harder to cut accurately—but that gives this mosaic its charm.

Ceramic, stone, and found objects can be heavy, so I highly recommend using a cement backer board for the substrate for this project.

Gears offer not only texture but metaphor, reminding viewers that soil teems with unseen activity.

Materials

- Cement backer board, 14 × 22 in., with hanger attached
- Ceramic
- Pebbles
- Found objects
- Sticky mesh
- Clear contact paper
- Thin-set mortar
- Cementitious grout
- Grout sealant

Tools

- Felt-tip marker
- Ceramic tile nipper
- Wet saw (optional)
- Painter's tape
- Dust mask
- Bucket
- Bowl
- Flat mixing trowel
- Notched metal trowel
- Rubber grout float
- Small painter's trowel
- Cotton cloths
- Small sponge

Template, page 285

1. **Secure the cartoon and sticky mesh to the substrate.** A word of caution: ceramic tiles are dusty and porous, which means that the sticky mesh doesn't grip them as well as it does glass tiles. However, the mesh still adds a modicum of control, so I recommend using it.

   Your cartoon should fit on the substrate, with a border of at least 1/8-in. between the edge of the cartoon and the edge of the substrate in order to leave enough space for a shoulder that will be grouted later. Lay the cartoon face-up on the substrate and place sticky mesh—sticky side up—on top of the cartoon. If the sticky mesh inhibits your view of the design, use a felt-tip marker to darken the lines of the cartoon. Then, tape down the corners with painter's tape to affix the cartoon and sticky mesh to the substrate so that your work surface and design will be secure and properly aligned while you lay the tiles.

2. **Lay in the found objects.** If you're using a ceramic watering can like the one in this mosaic, you'll need to prepare it beforehand. The watering can is hollow, so there's very little surface area on which to spread thin-set mortar, which will result in a weak adhesion to the substrate. To remedy this, fill the hollow space with thin-set mortar and a few ceramic pieces to create more surface area. Lay the watering can and any other three-dimensional objects in place on the sticky mesh.

3. **Dry lay the tesserae.** Working around the three-dimensional objects, dry lay the entire composition directly on the sticky mesh. When you get to the corners, remove the painter's tape so that the tesserae can properly adhere to the sticky mesh. Finalize the design at this stage and check the borders to ensure that no tesserae have crept over the edges of the cartoon. If they have, switch them out for smaller pieces to avoid creating a sharp edge or an insufficient shoulder for grouting.

4. **Cover the composition with contact paper.** First, remove the three-dimensional objects. Take a sheet of contact paper, slightly larger than the composition, and gently place it—sticky side down—on the surface of the mosaic, locking all the tesserae in place. Press the contact paper firmly onto each and every tessera, being mindful of the sharp edges under the contact paper. To avoid cutting yourself, use a balled-up cloth to press the tesserae down.

5. **Remove the composition from the substrate.** Before you can apply adhesive to the substrate, you must first remove the cartoon and sticky mesh from its surface. The easiest way to do this is with the aid of a flipper board—a board that you use to flip the composition over. The board can be any flat, lightweight board you have on hand—a spare piece of wood, plastic, or wedi board. As long as it's slightly larger than your mosaic, it will work.

   To safely remove your composition, place the flipper board on top of it. Hold both the top and bottom boards (the bottom being the substrate) securely—with the tesserae sandwiched safely in between—and simply flip them over. After you've executed the flip, your substrate will be on top of the pile. Remove it and face it right-side up on your work surface.

6. **Remove the cartoon and sticky mesh.** Remove the cartoon and gently pull the sticky mesh off the tesserae, being careful to pull slowly to avoid dislodging any tesserae from the contact paper underneath. Discard the sticky mesh.

7. **Apply thin-set mortar to the substrate.** Follow the directions in Preparing and Applying Thin-Set Mortar on page 42. Because ceramic tile is thicker than glass tile, it needs a slightly thicker bed of adhesive to hold it. When you're applying the thin-set mortar, use a lighter hand and leave a bit more thin-set on the substrate than you usually would to fully set the ceramic tile.

The pitcher now has adequate surface area to adhere to the substrate.

Dry lay the found object and mosaic around it.

The tesserae for this project were broken down from 4 × 4-in. ceramic tiles. The blue tiles are glazed, but the ones that comprise the ground are unglazed, which gives it a more earthy look.

To enhance the sense of depth, the color values are darker near the bottom of the mosaic.

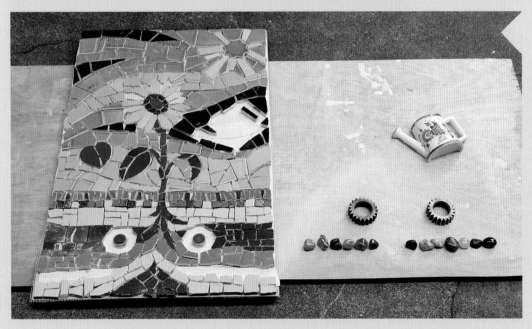

After you've laid the tesserae, remove the found objects and pebbles—anything that creates an uneven surface.

Unusually shaped objects, such as pebbles, should be hand-set into the mosaic.

Worn-out tools are given a second life in this Fix It mosaic, which is another example of how found objects can tell a story and show the maker's personality. In this instance, there's a fun literalism to it.

8. **Flip-and-set the composition back onto the substrate.** Follow the directions in step 7 of the Address Sign mosaic.

9. **Seat the tesserae.** Smooth down the entire composition through the contact paper, pressing each tessera into the thin-set mortar to ensure adhesion. Use a balled-up cloth during this process to avoid cutting yourself on any sharp edges. Place an even weight (such as a book) on the top of the mosaic to help the setting process, and let the mortar begin to cure for approximately 30 minutes. After 30 minutes, gently lift a corner of the contact paper. If you feel confident that you can pull away the contact paper without pulling up any tesserae, do so. The mortar will still be wet at this point, so if necessary you can do some final fine-tuning to the mosaic design.

10. **Hand-set the three-dimensional inclusions.** Using a small painter's trowel, butter the back of each object and press it firmly into the bed of thin-set.

11. **Clean up any extra adhesive.** The adhesive will be visible in the interstices. This is a problem only if it has squished up between the tesserae so much that it might block the grout. A good way to check for problem spots is to look at the contact paper after you pull it off—if it's spotted with mortar, the adhesive has risen above the level of the tesserae. If you see any problem spots, clean them out using a small painter's trowel or a thin piece of wire. Then let the thin-set mortar cure for 24 hours.

12. **Grout, polish, and seal the mosaic.** Follow the directions in Grouting Your Mosaic on page 49. For this piece, I used earthy red grout. It's a good complement to the subject matter.

This timeless timepiece reminds us of the sun's pivotal role in shaping and sustaining our environment.

Sundial

CHALLENGING

Sundials remind us of the sun's pivotal role in shaping the seasons and sustaining life. This mosaic is a lovely addition to a garden or patio—or anywhere that sees full sun.

The design of this mosaic pays homage to the sun and clouds, and the layout of the tesserae mimics the sun's rays; there's an outward trajectory from the gnomon that provides a lovely *andamento* to this piece. When you finish making your sundial, be sure to position it so that the gnomon points north (if you live in the Northern Hemisphere; point it south if you live in the Southern Hemisphere) so that it indicates the hour of the day accurately.

For details on how to calculate accurate lines for your cartoon and mosaic, visit www-spof.gsfc.nasa.gov/stargaze/Sundial.htm.

WHAT'S A GNOMON?

A gnomon is the pointer that casts a shadow on the sundial. Unlike the hands on a clock, the gnomon doesn't actually show you what time it is. Rather, as the sun crosses the sky, the gnomon's shadow sweeps across the face of the sundial, showing you how many hours of sun are left in the day.

The gnomon is positioned parallel to the North Pole, so the angle of the gnomon depends on the latitude of your location. Portland, Oregon, where I live, is 45-degrees latitude, so the gnomon in this project is bent at a 45-degree angle. Los Angeles is at 34-degrees latitude, so if you live in Los Angeles, you'd use a gnomon with a 34-degree angle. To determine the angle of your gnomon, you'll need to know the latitude of your location. You can find a sundial calculator online—you input your latitude and it calculates the measurements and tells you where to draw the hour lines on your sundial. Use a protractor for accurate angles.

Materials

- 14½ × 3-in.-deep potting tray
- Cooking spray
- Metal rod, 22 in. long and ⅜ in. wide
- Portland cement
- Sand
- Wood support (2 × 6-in. block cut at a 45-degree angle and a 16-in. strip of plywood)
- Chicken wire (cut about 1 in. smaller in diameter than the sundial container)
- Stained glass
- Sticky mesh
- Clear contact paper
- Thin-set mortar
- Cementitious grout
- Grout sealant
- Newspaper to protect work surface from concrete

Tools

- Felt-tip marker
- Pistol-grip glass cutter
- Glass runner
- Two-wheeled nipper
- 12 × 12 board (for sliding the mosaic onto the substrate)
- Protractor
- Plastic trowel
- Painter's tape
- Dust mask
- Bowl
- Flat mixing trowel
- Notched metal trowel
- Rubber grout float
- Small painter's trowel
- Cotton cloths
- Small sponge
- 2 mixing buckets (2.5 gallon)

Template, page 286

Some basic materials for the sundial mosaic: a circular form (potting tray; this one is plastic), chicken wire, gnomon, and an angled wooden piece to support the gnomon during the setting process.

MIXING CONCRETE

You can mix concrete yourself, or you can buy premixed concrete. I prefer to mix my own, because it gives me more control over the consistency. Also, premixed concrete contains gravel, which makes it chunkier and therefore less desirable if you want a smooth consistency for a mosaic. If you opt for premixed concrete, you can strain some of the gravel out. In either case, wear a dust mask, because the process is dusty. Also, spread some newspaper or a tarp underneath the bucket to protect your work surface.

Materials
- Portland cement
- Sand
- Water

Tools
- Dust mask
- Latex gloves
- Bucket
- Flat mixing trowel

To mix your own concrete, first put on your gloves and mask. Combine the sand and Portland cement in dry form in a 3:1 ratio in a bucket (3 parts sand to 1 part cement). Stir until they're well combined. Then slowly add water in a 1:1 ratio to the amount of dry cement. For example, 3 parts sand, 1 part dry cement, 1 part water. Stir the mixture with a flat mixing trowel. The concrete should be thick but fluid (more fluid than thin-set mortar or grout). If it's runny, it's too wet. If you're using premixed concrete, follow the manufacturer's instructions.

1. **Mix the concrete.** To estimate how much cement to mix, scoop cement and sand into the container you'll use for the project in a 3:1 ratio (3 parts sand to 1 part cement) until it's almost full (the mixture should be about ½ in. from the top of the container). Then carefully transfer the cement and sand to a mixing bucket and begin mixing, following the directions in Mixing Concrete.

2. **Pour the concrete into the potting tray and secure the gnomon.** Spray the inside of the potting tray with cooking spray—the coating of spray makes it easier to remove the hardened concrete later. Pour about a third of the concrete into the container and place the

chicken wire on top of the concrete. (The chicken wire provides structural strength to the concrete and prevents it from cracking.) Set the gnomon in place, with the corner that's bent positioned about 2 inches from the side of the container. Pour in enough concrete to fill the container to the top. Support the gnomon with the wood block so that it won't tilt. If you feel that the gnomon isn't stabilizing, then support it on each side with pieces of tile or thick metal bolts as you are filling the tray with concrete. Tamp down the concrete with a plastic trowel as you pour, leaving a slight mound in the center so that rain won't collect on the sundial (you might have to pour in a bit more concrete to the middle and smooth it). Patience is key in this step: the concrete becomes harder over time, so the longer you can wait for the gnomon to stabilize the better.

3. **Wait for the concrete to cure.** To help support the gnomon as the concrete dries, lay a piece of plywood across the surface of the tray. Tuck a wedge of wood under the gnomon. For best results, wait 48 to 72 hours for the concrete to fully harden after you've poured it. You can begin working on the mosaic while you're waiting for the concrete to dry.

4. **Clean up and dispose of excess concrete.** Don't pour or rinse any concrete down a drain. Instead, pour leftover concrete into the garbage.

5. **Secure the cartoon and sticky mesh to a temporary substrate.** Make a cartoon that's the size and shape of the sundial surface, with a section cut out for the gnomon, and work on a temporary substrate, such as a piece of wood or wedi board. (You will use the slide-and-set technique to set the mosaic around the gnomon.) Keep in mind that you'll need a border of at least ⅛ in. between the edge of the cartoon and the edge of the substrate in order to leave enough space for a shoulder that will be grouted later.

Lay the cartoon face-up on the temporary substrate and place sticky mesh—sticky side up—on top of the cartoon. If the sticky mesh inhibits your view of the design, use a marker to darken the lines of the cartoon. Then, tape down the edges with painter's tape to affix the cartoon and sticky mesh to the temporary substrate so that your work surface and design will be secure and properly aligned while you lay the tiles.

6. **Dry lay the tesserae.** Dry lay the entire composition directly on the sticky mesh over the cartoon. When you get to the taped edges, remove the painter's tape so that the tesserae can properly adhere to the sticky mesh. Finalize the design at this stage and check the borders to ensure that no tesserae have crept over the edges of the cartoon. If they have, switch them out for smaller pieces to avoid creating a sharp edge or an insufficient shoulder for grouting.

7. **Cover the composition with contact paper.** Take a sheet of contact paper, slightly larger than the composition, and make a cut in it to accommodate the gnomon. Gently place the contact paper—sticky side down—on the surface of the mosaic, locking all the tesserae in place. Press the contact paper firmly onto each and every tessera, being mindful of the sharp edges under the contact paper. To avoid cutting yourself, use a balled-up cloth to press the tesserae down.

8. **Remove the composition from the temporary substrate.** The easiest way to do this is with the aid of a flipper board—a board that you use to flip the composition over. The board can be any flat, lightweight board you have on hand—a spare piece of wood, plastic, or wedi board. As long as it's slightly larger than your mosaic, it will work.

   To safely remove your composition, place the flipper board on top of it. Hold both the top and bottom boards (the bottom being

Place chicken wire on the first layer of concrete, then pour the remaining concrete and set the gnomon.

If the gnomon isn't stabilizing, brace it on both sides (laterally) with pieces of ceramic tile (like the small white rectangular pieces seen in the cement) or thick metal bolts.

The gnomon is supported by a piece of plywood across the surface of the tray and a wedge of wood tucked into the angle.

To leave room for the gnomon in the mosaic's design, a small piece has been cut out of the cartoon and sticky mesh.

the temporary substrate) securely—with the tesserae sandwiched safely in between—and simply flip them over. After you've executed the flip, the temporary substrate will be on top of the pile. Remove it, and then remove the cartoon and pull the sticky mesh off carefully. Now place another board, or the temporary substrate, if it's suitable, on top of the composition, hold the two boards together firmly, and flip them so that the composition is right-side up. Leave the mosaic on the board—you'll slide it off in step 10.

9. **Apply thin-set mortar to the poured concrete.** Follow the directions in Preparing and Applying Thin-Set Mortar on page 42.

10. **Slide-and-set the composition on top of the concrete.** Measuring with your eyes, line up the composition with the substrate. Remove

Remove any tesserae that might get in the way of sliding the composition easily onto the thin-set mortar.

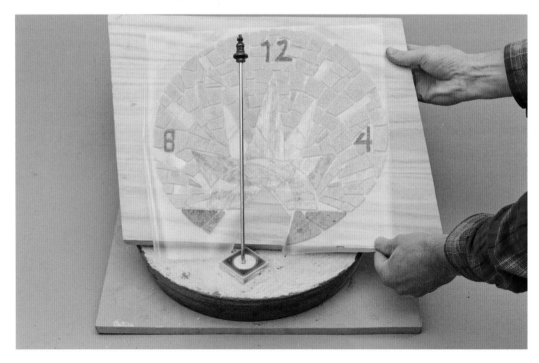

any tiles that might get in the way of an easy slide onto the thin-set mortar. Slide the mosaic directly onto the substrate, pulling away the board as you go. Once you've set the mosaic down, you can shift it more precisely into place so that it's centered on the substrate. If any tesserae popped off the contact paper, fit them back into the design. Let the mortar begin to cure for approximately 30 minutes. After 30 minutes, gently lift a corner of the contact paper. If you feel confident that you can pull away the contact paper without pulling up any tesserae, do so. The mortar will still be wet at this point, so if necessary you can do some final fine-tuning to the mosaic design. Let the thin-set mortar cure for 24 hours.

11. **Grout, polish, and seal the mosaic.** Follow the directions in Grouting Your Mosaic on page 49.

12. **Remove the sundial from the container.** Pick up the container and push gently on the bottom with your fingers, using your thumbs to hold the rim. The poured form should pop away from the container. Before it pops out completely, place one hand on top of the mosaic and the other underneath the container and carefully turn the form over into one hand as you pull the container away with the other hand.

This earthy pebble mosaic fits seamlessly into a garden.

Pebble Stepping-Stone

EASY

Materials

- 12 × 12-in. wooden form (see Make a Wooden Form)
- River rock in two colors and of equal sizes, approximately 1 × 2 × ½ in.
- 5-in.-diameter concrete pipe
- Chicken wire, 11 × 11 in.
- Sand
- Portland cement

Tools

- Wet saw
- Plastic trowel
- Spoon
- 2½-gallon bucket
- Wire brush
- Plywood (a bit smaller than 12 × 12)

Template, page 287

This pebble stepping-stone is a departure from the other projects in this book, because it's created using the reverse method, an ancient mosaic technique that is rarely used now. With the reverse method, you dry lay the tesserae upside-down in a bed of sand and then pour concrete over the tesserae. When the concrete cures, you turn the mosaic over, hose off the sand, and voilà—you can see your design. There is a bit of setup for this project, but the process moves quickly after the initial preparation. I used salvaged 5-in. concrete pipes for this project; if you can't find concrete pipes, try using curved ceramic roof tiles—you'll want to use something with a built-in curve.

1. **Construct a square wooden form.** Follow the directions in Make a Wooden Form.

2. **Pour a half-inch layer of sand into the form.**

3. **Lay the tesserae.** Use the photos of this mosaic as a reference for how to arrange the pipes and pebbles. Push the pipes into the sand first; push them down until you feel them touch the wood base. Then push the thin edge of each pebble into the sand until the pebble touches the bottom of the form. This will ensure that your

MAKE A WOODEN FORM

Materials

- 15 × 15-in. piece of ⅝-in.-thick plywood (for the base)
- Two 2 × 4 × 15-in. pieces of plywood (for the sides)
- Two 2 × 4 × 12-in. pieces of plywood (for the sides)
- 1½-in. screws
- 2½-in. screws

Tools

- Duct tape
- Drill or screwdriver

Use 2½-in. screws to secure the sides together in a square. Then, screw the base to the sides, using twelve 1½-in. screws. Use duct tape to tape the seams on the inside of the form along the bottom and up the sides to prevent sand and water from leaking out.

This simple wooden box creates a form in which you'll seat the tesserae and pour the concrete. The dimensions are 15 × 15 in. on the outer edge and 12 × 12 in. on the inside. In this upside-down view, you can see where to insert the screws.

⅝-in. plywood

2 × 4 in 12- and 15-in. lengths

CUTTING CEMENT PIPES

The curved pieces in this mosaic are actually old concrete pipes that have been cut in thirds and given a new life as tesserae. Cutting the pipes requires a wet saw. Take a 6-in. length of pipe and cut it into thirds. Then, cut each of those pieces on the cross section; the width should be equal to that of your pebbles. The pebbles I used in this mosaic are about 1 in. wide, so I cut the cross sections into 1-in. segments.

Use a wet saw to cut cement pipes.

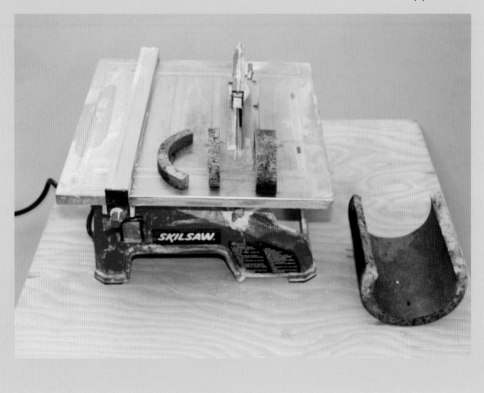

Sand will displace as you work; scoop out any excess with a spoon—the sand should only cover the bottom half of the pebbles.

Here's the finished setting—the wood form, the cement pipe pieces, the pebbles, and the sand, ready to be covered with a layer of concrete.

The first layer of concrete covered with a piece of chicken wire.

mosaic will have a level surface when it's turned over. The sand should only cover the bottom half of the pebbles. Use a spoon to scoop out some of the sand if necessary.

4. **Prepare and pour the concrete base.** To mix the concrete, follow the directions in Mixing Concrete on page 187. However, use a bit more water to make the mix more fluid. Set the form on a level surface. Slowly pour a layer of concrete over the pebbles and sand until the pebbles are just covered. Tamp down the concrete gently, making sure that it fills in between all the pebbles. Then lay a piece of chicken wire on the concrete. (The chicken wire provides structural strength to the concrete and prevents it from cracking.) Pour a layer of concrete over the chicken wire, filling the form until the concrete is ¼ in. from the top edge. Using a plastic trowel, tamp down the concrete again.

5. **Let the concrete cure for 72 hours.** Put some newspaper underneath the form to absorb any moisture that seeps out.

6. **Remove the wooden form.** Once the concrete has cured, place the piece of plywood on top of the poured concrete. Holding the plywood and form together, turn wood form upside down so that the concrete sits on the plywood. Remove the screws from the sides and base of the form and remove the pieces of the form. Turn the mosaic right-side up. Spray off the sand with a garden hose, and use a wire brush to sweep away any excess sand.

Mosaic transforms a humble planter into a work of art.

Planter with Mosaic Frieze

MODERATE

Materials
- Container
- Stained glass
- Sticky mesh
- Clear contact paper
- Thin-set mortar
- Cementitious grout
- Grout sealant

Tools
- Ruler
- Pencil
- Pistol-grip glass cutter
- Two-wheeled nippers
- Glass runner
- Painter's tape
- 12 × 30-in. board (for sliding the mosaic onto the substrate)
- Dust mask
- Bucket
- Bowl
- Flat mixing trowel
- Notched metal trowel
- Small painter's trowel
- Rubber grout float
- Cotton cloths
- Small sponge

Template, page 288

If you want to jazz up your container garden or potted plants, a planter with a mosaic frieze will give them some added style. You can mosaic many different container shapes, but keep in mind that curved surfaces create more of a technical challenge—you'll need to use narrow tiles around the curves; wide tiles won't adhere to a curved surface. The planter shown here is 16 × 36 in., so it had long, flat sides that were easy to work with. I used the double-direct-with-slide method on the long sides, and set the tiles on the curved ends directly.

The design consists of four vignettes—three vignettes of the same design for both of the long sides and one vignette on each end. I used garden imagery on the side vignettes and a simple circle on the end vignettes. The horizontal border creates a clean line and a strong wrapping effect.

1. **Apply a scratch coat to the planter where the mosaic for the first side vignette will be placed.** The scratch coat will guide you when it comes time to set your composition. Tape your cartoon to the planter, and use a ruler to ensure that the space between the top of the

cartoon and the lip of the container is even. Trace around the cartoon with a pencil. Continue the top horizontal line all the way around the container; it will act as a guide for setting the remaining vignettes. Remove the cartoon and apply a scratch coat of thin-set mortar to the area you've outlined. Let scratch coat cure for 24 hours.

2. **Secure the cartoon and sticky mesh to a temporary substrate.** Lay the cartoon face-up on the temporary substrate and place sticky mesh—sticky side up—on top of the cartoon. If the sticky mesh inhibits your view of the design, use a marker to darken the lines of the cartoon. Then, tape down the corners with painter's tape to affix the cartoon and sticky mesh to the substrate so that your work surface and design will be secure and properly aligned while you lay the tiles.

3. **Dry lay the tesserae for the side vignette.** Dry lay the design for the side vignette directly on the sticky mesh over the cartoon. When you get to the corners, remove the painter's tape so that the tesserae can properly adhere to the sticky mesh. Finalize the design at this stage and check the borders to ensure that no tesserae have crept over the edges of the cartoon. If they have, switch them out for smaller pieces to avoid creating a sharp edge or an insufficient shoulder for grouting.

4. **Cover the composition with contact paper.** Take a sheet of contact paper, slightly larger than the composition, and gently place it—sticky side down—on the surface of the mosaic, locking all the tesserae in place. Press the contact paper firmly onto each and every tessera, being mindful of the sharp edges under the contact paper. To avoid cutting yourself, use a balled-up cloth to press the tesserae down. The side panel will be set with the double-direct-with-slide method.

5. **Remove the composition from the temporary substrate.** The easiest way to do this is with the aid of a flipper board—a board that you use to flip the composition over. The board can be any flat, lightweight board you have on hand—a spare piece of wood, plastic, or wedi board. As long as it's slightly larger than your mosaic, it will work.

    To safely remove your composition, place the flipper board on top of it. Hold both the top and bottom boards (the bottom being the temporary substrate) securely—with the tesserae sandwiched safely in between—and simply flip them over. After you've executed the flip, your temporary substrate will be on top of the pile. Remove it, and then remove the cartoon and pull the sticky mesh off carefully.

6. **Apply thin-set mortar on top of the scratch coat.** Follow the directions in Preparing and Applying Thin-Set Mortar on page 42.

7. **Slide-and-set the side vignette onto the substrate.** Set the container on its side and use stacks of magazines to hold it steady if necessary. Carefully pick up the segment and place it on the slider board, right-side up. Measuring with your eye, line up the composition segment with its matching area on the substrate. Slide the mosaic directly onto the substrate, pulling away the board as you go.

8. **Seat the tesserae.** Smooth down the entire composition through the contact paper, pressing each tessera into the thin-set mortar to ensure adhesion. Use a balled-up cloth during this process to avoid cutting yourself on any sharp edges. Let the mortar begin to cure for approximately 30 minutes. After 30 minutes, gently lift a corner of the contact paper. If you feel confident that you can pull away the contact paper without pulling up any tesserae, do so. The mortar will still be wet at this point, so if necessary you can do some final fine-tuning to the mosaic design.

Terra-cotta is popular as a mosaic substrate, but it's prone to cracking in freeze-thaw cycles. To make a lasting piece for your garden, choose a container made of a durable material, such as lightweight fiberglass cement or high-fire terra-cotta. Alternatively, bring the planter inside during winter.

Tape your cartoon to the planter and trace around it with a pencil.

Fill in the outline of the cartoon with a scratch coat of thin-set mortar. A scratch coat is a helpful guide when you're only mosaicking a portion of a substrate.

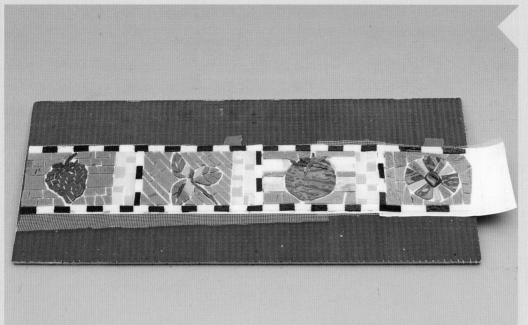

Working on a temporary substrate, I laid the three side vignettes, plus one of the end pieces (the circular design on the right). The bold black-and-white pattern makes a fantastic border for this mosaic.

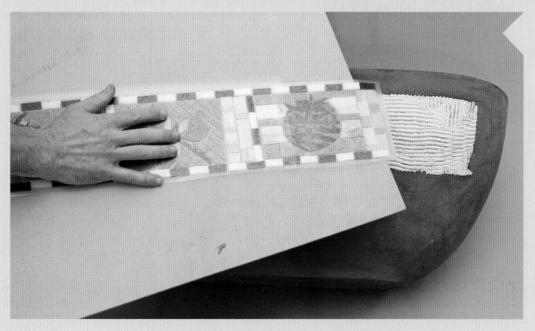

Use the slide technique to set the mosaic in place.

Use the direct method to set the end vignette. Notice how I'm staying within the outline that I drew earlier.

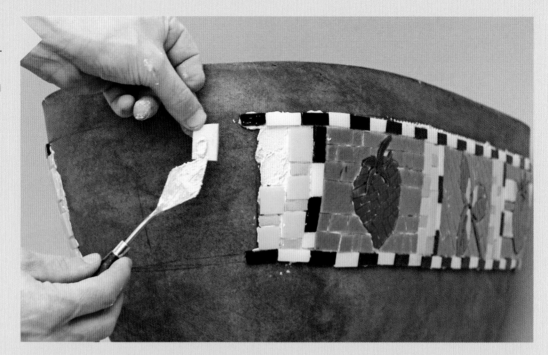

Here, I'm beginning to grout, and I've applied painter's tape around the edges of the mosaic, leaving ⅛ in. of space between the mosaic edge and the tape in order to create a shoulder.

9. **Clean up any extra adhesive.** The adhesive will be visible in the interstices. This is a problem only if it has squished up between the tesserae so much that it might block the grout. A good way to check for problem spots is to look at the contact paper after you pull it off—if it's spotted with mortar, the adhesive has risen above the level of the tesserae. If you see any problem spots, clean them out using a small painter's trowel or a thin piece of wire. Then let the thin-set mortar cure for 24 hours.

10. **Repeat steps 1 through 9 for the vignette on the other side of the planter.**

11. **Use the direct method to hand-set both of the end vignettes.** Follow the directions in steps 2 and 3. Use a small painter's trowel to apply thin-set to the container and to butter the back of each tessera. Press each tessera firmly into the thin-set.

12. **Clean up any extra adhesive in the end vignettes.** Follow the directions in step 9.

13. **Grout, polish, and seal the mosaic.** Follow the directions in Grouting Your Mosaic on page 49, but first, tape around the edges of the mosaic, leaving an eighth of an inch between the tape and the edge of the composition to allow space for a neat shoulder. When you're grouting, try not to get too much grout on the tape—you'll risk pulling up the grouted shoulder when you pull the tape away.

Doesn't the jeweled frog look right at home, perched amidst the plants?

Jeweled Frog Planter

EASY

For this project, I used a terra-cotta frog planter that I found at an import shop that sells Mexican pottery. Terra-cotta is not as hardy as the other substrates used in this book—it's prone to cracking during freeze-thaw cycles—so be sure to bring it indoors during frosty weather.

Designing a contoured three-dimensional mosaic is tricky, but here's a tip: take a photo of the form and print out a few copies. Draw your designs on the photos to experiment with different ideas. Once you've finalized the design, you can use a permanent marker to draw it directly on the surface of the form.

The contours of the planter will guide your work, and you can use tesserae of various colors and shapes to highlight them. For this piece, I used different shades of green, which seemed appropriate for a frog, along with some browns and yellows for contrast. Flat-back marbles give the frog its bejeweled appearance.

When you cut your bank of tesserae, cut a supply of small pieces too—you'll need them to mosaic around the contours of the form. This is a mosaic that is likely to be touched, so I recommend using a rock tumbler to soften the edges of the tesserae.

Materials

- Terra-cotta frog planter
- Stained-glass tesserae, run through a rock tumbler
- Small flat-back marbles
- Thin-set mortar
- Cementitious grout
- Grout sealant

Tools

- Rock tumbler
- Permanent marker
- Pistol-grip glass cutter
- Glass runner
- Two-wheeled nipper
- Painter's tape
- Dust mask
- Bucket
- Bowl
- Flat mixing trowel
- Rubber grout float
- Plastic sandwich bag
- Small painter's trowel
- Cotton cloths
- Small sponge
- Tweezers
- Latex gloves

Photographs are a handy design aid, because you can sketch different ideas on them until you finalize a concept.

With a scratch coat and drawn-on design, the frog is ready to go.

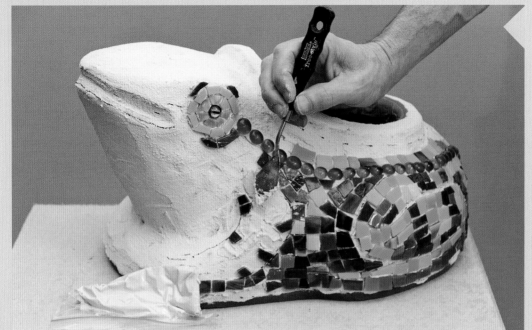

Work in the direct method for this project, and use a sandwich bag as a makeshift piping bag. It's helpful to have a small trowel on hand for smoothing the thin-set mortar and buttering the back of tesserae.

Different color values help distinguish between the frog's body and limbs. The marbles are wartlike and dimensional, and they brighten up the piece.

The earthy, red-brown grout preserves the look of the original terra-cotta container, as well as being a nice complement to the green tesserae.

ROCK TUMBLERS

For any mosaic that might be handled or touched, use a rock tumbler to smooth the edges of the tesserae. I use a small rock tumbler with steel shot the size of BB's. You can buy a rock tumbler at any rock and gem store. I fill the bottom level of the tumbler with steel shot and then add the cut glass tesserae just past the half-way point of the tumbler. Finally, I add water to cover the tesserae. Then I firmly attach the top and run the tumbler for 90 minutes. Drain the water in the sink and let the tesserae dry on a cloth.

1. **Prepare the planter with a scratch coat.** Tape the inside edge of the opening with painter's tape. Using a rubber grout float, apply a layer of thin-set mortar to the entire area to be mosaicked. This will create a stronger surface, which will help the terra-cotta withstand moisture, as well as smoothing out any uneven spots on the planter's surface.

2. **Transfer the design to the substrate.** After the scratch coat has dried, use a marker to draw the design directly on the surface of the frog.

3. **Hand-set the tesserae using the direct method.** Prepare a batch thin-set mortar by following the directions in Preparing and Applying Thin-Set Mortar on page 42, but do not apply the mortar according to those directions. Working on one section at a time, use a small painter's trowel to spread thin-set mortar to a small area of the frog. Then place thin-set mortar on the back of each tessera by using the same small painter's trowel or using a sandwich bag with a corner snipped off as a makeshift piping bag. Hand-set each tessera, pressing them firmly into the thin-set. Let the thin-set mortar cure for 24 hours.

4. **Grout, polish, and seal the mosaic.** Follow the directions in Grouting Your Mosaic on page 49. If you have trouble getting the grout around all the contours, put on a pair of latex gloves and fine-tune the grout by hand.

This colorful piece offers a bright and modern take on the classic pagoda form. The top is removable, and the interior is hollow, with room for a candle to be inserted and lit.

Pagoda

MODERATE

This mosaic puts a distinctive spin on a store-bought cement pagoda, which you can find at garden-supply stores. I had a lot of fun with color here, but the strong black outlines hold the piece together visually.

Like the frog planter project, this is a project for which you might want to sketch some designs on photographs before committing to one. Decide on a color scheme beforehand and make a bank of stained-glass tesserae to draw from. Consider how the contours of the onion-shaped top of the pagoda will affect the design. The form will influence where you put the grout lines. Don't use large tesserae on the top—they won't adhere to the curves; you'll need to use small tesserae. I used mostly squares and rectangles, with a little variety thrown in here and there. Work in the direct method, section by section, adhering the tesserae as you go along. This is a mosaic that is likely to be touched, so I recommend using a rock tumbler to soften the edges of the tesserae.

Strong black lines emphasize the pagoda's contours, leaving you with plenty of room to play with color. Flat-back marbles provide variety and added flourish.

Materials

- Precast cement pagoda
- Stained-glass tesserae, run through a rock tumbler
- Flat-back marbles
- Thin-set mortar
- Cementitious grout
- Grout sealant

Tools

- Rock tumbler
- Felt-tip marker
- Pistol-grip glass cutter
- Glass runner
- Two-wheeled nipper
- Painter's tape
- Sandwich bag
- Tweezers
- Dust mask
- Bucket
- Bowl
- Flat mixing trowel
- Rubber grout float
- Small painter's trowel
- Cotton cloths
- Small sponge
- Latex gloves

1. **Prepare the Pagoda surface for tiling.** Sometimes the surfaces of a precast form are rough so that it is a good idea to apply a smooth layer of thin-set mortar (follow the instructions on pages 42–43). Use a rubber grout float to apply the mortar. Let this set for 24 hours before beginning the mosaic.

2. **Hand-set the tesserae using the direct method.** Set the outlines of your design on the pagoda surface. Working on a small section at a time, use a small painter's trowel to spread thin-set mortar on the area. Hand-set each tessera, being sure to butter the back before pressing it firmly into the thin-set. If you like, tilt the pagoda on its side for easier access. Leave the lower part of the legs bare; they'll settle into the ground, so it's not worth the effort to mosaic them. For hard-to-reach places, I often use tweezers to help set the tesserae. Let the thin-set mortar cure for 24 hours.

3. **Grout, polish, and seal the mosaic.** Follow the directions in Grouting Your Mosaic on page 49, but first use painter's tape to cover any exposed edges (such as the bottom part of the legs and window ledges) that you don't want colored by stray grout. Because the pagoda has so many edges, allow extra time for grouting. You may need to work over the course of two sessions.

The strong black lines emphasize the contours of the pagoda.

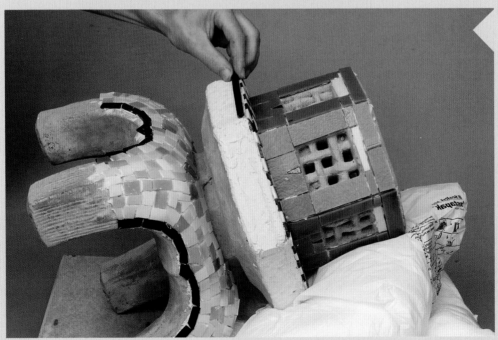

Tilting the pagoda gives you a flat surface that's easier to tile.

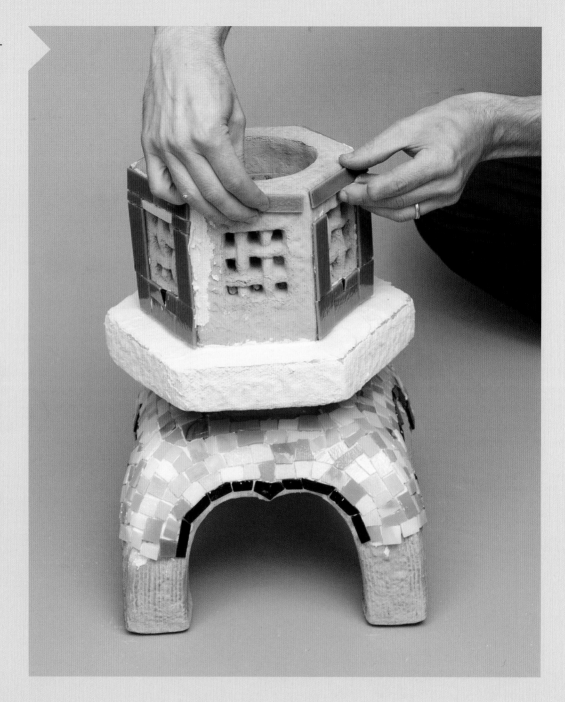

Leave ample room (approximately ⅛ in.) at the corners for grout.

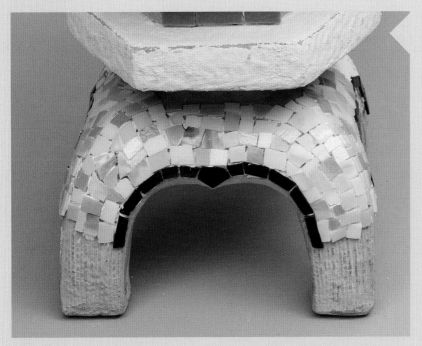

The legs have a lot of color, but the colors are all the same value, so they don't fight each other for prominence in the viewer's eye.

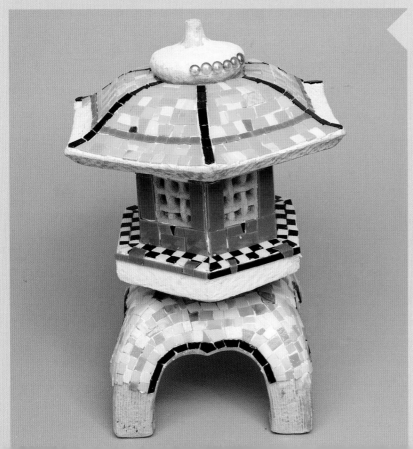

I emphasized the floor in the middle by using a checkerboard pattern. Also, I tested colors for the border of the middle level by first taping up two different colors of tile—one brown, one black—to see which looked best. I choose the black tile because I wanted the edge of the sides to connect to the design that was immediately above, to make the levels look more solid.

This ambitious centerpiece will wow visitors—both human and feathered!

Blooming Birdbath

CHALLENGING

Materials

- Concrete birdbath
- Stained glass
- Thin-set adhesive
- Urethane grout

Tools

- Rock tumbler
- Pistol-grip glass cutter
- Glass runner
- Two-wheeled nipper
- Permanent marker
- Dust mask
- Bucket
- Bowl
- Flat mixing trowel
- Sandwich bag
- Rubber grout float
- Small painter's trowel
- Cotton cloths
- Small sponge

The inspiration for this mosaic design came directly from the birdbath itself—the contours of the basin are reminiscent of flower petals, so I decided to make a blooming birdbath. This classic garden centerpiece will catch the eye of both human and feathered friends.

You can find birdbaths at most garden-supply centers. Since the basin and the base are two pieces, treat them as separate yet coordinating mosaics when you create your design.

Use a rock tumbler to take the sharp edges off the tesserae that you plan on using for the edges and base, since children might touch it. I chose to use a sand-colored urethane grout to unify the design and maintain a light feel. Plus, the grout will inevitably get dirty from the exposure to water—a sand-colored grout will help mask the dirt.

1. **Draw your design directly on the basin.**

2. **Hand-set the basin using the direct method.** Follow the directions in Preparing and Applying Thin-Set Mortar on page 42. Working in small segments, use a trowel to spread thin-set adhesive on the immediate area. Hand-set each tessera, being sure to butter the back before pressing it firmly into the thin-set.

Here, you can see the gradation of the colors in the petals—the lightest colors are on the highest part of the edge, working down to the deeper orange, which shows some depth. I like taking two different pieces of glass and blending them together to show a color or value change. I outlined the petals in purple to distinguish them with a complementary color.

I included green on the basin because I knew the base of the birdbath would likely incorporate a lot of green. The pinwheel shape creates the impression of a domelike center.

A bird's-eye view of the basin. You can see the appealing contrast between the yellow and orange petals and the rich purple border.

The fluted base has many small planes. Line up the tesserae so that the grout lines align with the edges of the fluted sections. I set up a temporary structure using a sawhorse and scraps of wood so that the base could rest in a tilted position for easier tiling.

Once the stems and grass were completed, I filled in the background with a lighter value. It's easiest to use tesserae that fit within the edges of the fluting.

3. **Draw your design on the base.** To design the base, reattach the basin so you can visualize how the two will work together. When you settle on a design, transfer it to the base of the birdbath.

4. **Hand-set the base using the direct method.**

5. **Grout the mosaic with urethane grout.** Urethane grout has a built-in adhesive to make it stronger, and it provides a watertight seal, so it's a must-have for a birdbath. It tends to dry fast and is harder to clean, so it's best to grout and clean one section of the mosaic at a time, in less than 15 minutes each. Grout an area that is approximately 10 × 10 in., then stop grouting and use a damp sponge to clean the grouted area. Scrub repeatedly in a circular motion to get the excess grout off the mosaic surface. (You need to use more elbow grease when you're working with urethane grout.) After you've cleaned the area, proceed with the next section of the mosaic.

I took a photo of the base and printed it out and drew several design ideas on it before settling on one I liked.

With a boldly contoured face and flaming hair, the design of the mosaic echoes both the form and function of the chimenea.

Chimenea

CHALLENGING

Materials

- Chimenea
- Stained glass
- Fused-glass tesserae for the eyes
- Sticky mesh
- Clear contact paper
- Thin-set mortar
- Cementitious grout
- Grout sealant

Tools

- Rock tumbler
- Felt-tip marker
- Pistol-grip glass cutter
- Glass runner
- Two-wheeled nipper
- Utility knife
- Painter's tape
- Dust mask
- Bucket
- Bowl
- Flat mixing trowel
- Notched metal trowel
- Rubber grout float
- Sandwich bag
- Small painter's trowel
- Cotton cloths
- Small sponge

Templates, pages 289, 290

A chimenea is a cozy focal point and gathering space in a garden. Adding a mosaic to the chimenea just makes it that much better!

The design here was inspired, of course, by fire. I added a friendly face with flamelike hair on the back side and a cloud of smoke in the shape of a heart on the side with the opening. I left some of the terracotta exposed for two reasons: first, because I like the way it looks, and second, because it would have been too time-intensive to mosaic the entire chimenea. I used the direct method (because of the contours) and the drape-and-set method to seat the tesserae for this project. Like some of the other mosaics in this book, this is a mosaic that is likely to be touched, so I recommend using a rock tumbler to soften the edges of the tesserae. Terra-cotta is a great mosaic substrate, but it's prone to cracking in freeze-thaw cycles, so bring your chimenea indoors during the winter.

1. **Create three cartoons.** This design is comprised of three separate yet coordinated mosaics: the face and hair on the back side and the smoke on the front. Each piece requires a cartoon of its own.

   Face Make paper stencils for the eyes, nose, and mouth, and use them to experiment with your design directly on the surface of the chimenea. This will help you get a sense of how the chimenea's

When you're considering colors, use at least four tones for the skin to create contours on the face, and choose a grout color that will blend well with the skin tone of the face.

curved form will affect the layout of the face. Move the features around on the surface of the chimenea until you're happy with their positions, then trace around the stencils directly onto the chimenea. Complete the design by drawing eyebrows and outlining the contours of the face. Transfer the design from the surface of the chimenea to a full-scale template to work on a flat surface.

Hair Use the template on page 290, or make a flame-shaped stencil from a piece of paper. Tape the stencil to the stack. Be sure that the flames do not curve too much around the side of the stack, as tight curve creates technical difficulties. Design flames that shoot upward rather than around.

Smoke The front of the chimenea features smoke in the shape of a heart, as well as a simple patterned border around the mouth of the firebox. Cut out a paper stencil for the smoke cloud and trace it onto the substrate.

2. **Add a scratch coat of thin-set mortar.** Apply a scratch coat of thin-set mortar to the area where the face will be set. Follow the directions in Preparing and Applying Thin-Set Mortar on page 42. Repeat this step for the hair and face when you're ready to set them.

3. **Secure the cartoons and sticky mesh to a temporary substrate.** Lay the cartoons face-up on the temporary substrate and place a piece of sticky mesh—sticky side up—on top of each cartoon. If the sticky mesh inhibits your view of the design, use a marker to darken the lines of the cartoon. Then, tape down the edges with painter's tape to affix the cartoon and sticky mesh to the temporary substrate so that your work surface and design will be secure and properly aligned while you lay the tiles.

To help you visualize your design, tape stencils for the face and flame to the work surface.

Here, I've begun setting the features, starting with the fused-glass eyes. I used at least four tones for the skin color to show contouring on the face.

Here is the flamelike hair, dry laid on sticky mesh. The black lines show where I cut the composition into five segments. Separating the composition into segments gives you smaller, narrower pieces to work with, making it easier to set the composition on the curved surface of the chimenea.

I used the direct method to adhere the smoke-shaped heart to the chimenea. It's handy to have the composition dry laid on sticky mesh on a table next to you before transferring it to the chimenea—it speeds up the setting process considerably.

I added black lines to highlight the cheeks and outlined the face with a slightly darker tone to show contour. I wrapped some hair around the side of the face to unify the hair and face.

Wrapping the hair around the sides of the mosaic helps to connect the front and back of the design.

This is the chimenea's big mouth. You can see the hair wrapping around the side and the simple pattern of three alternating colors that I used around the mouth. The dark lines in the white background symbolize the threads of smoke going up in a heart shape.

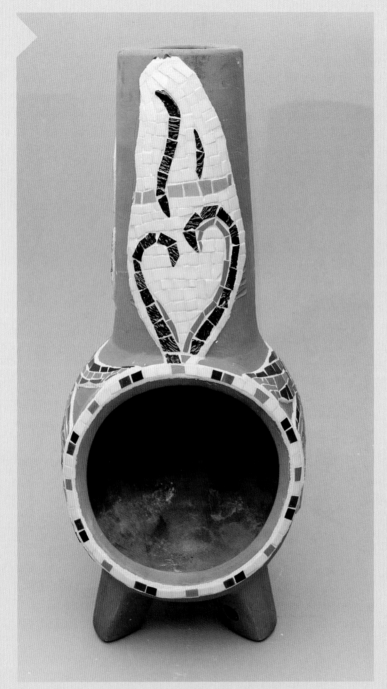

4. **Dry lay the tesserae for all three compositions.** Dry lay the three compositions directly on the sticky mesh over their cartoons. When you get to the edges, remove the painter's tape so that the tesserae can properly adhere to the sticky mesh. Finalize the design at this stage and check the borders to ensure that no tesserae have crept over the edges of the cartoon. If they have, switch them out for smaller pieces to avoid creating a sharp edge.

5. **Hand-set the face and smoke using the direct method.** Working on a small area at a time, use a small painter's trowel to spread thin-set mortar on the area you're working on. When you set the face, set the fused-glass eyes first. Hand-set each tessera, being sure to butter the back of it with thin-set before pressing it firmly into the thin-set. For quick buttering, fill a sandwich bag with thin-set and cut off one corner to create a makeshift piping bag. Hold the piping bag in one hand and squeeze a dollop of thin-set onto the back of each tessera before you seat it.

6. **Add a border to the firebox.** Using the direct method, hand-set a simple pattern around the mouth of the firebox. For design continuity, carry over the color scheme from the smoke heart.

7. **Prepare the flame for drape-and-set.** Unlike the other two portions of this mosaic, which were set using the direct method, it's more expedient to use the drape-and-set method for the flame. Take a sheet of contact paper, slightly larger than your composition, and gently place it—sticky side down—on the surface of the mosaic, locking all the tesserae in place. Press the contact paper firmly onto each and every tessera, being mindful of the sharp edges under the contact paper. To avoid cutting yourself, use a balled-up cloth to press the tesserae down. Then, using a utility knife, carefully cut the composition through the contact paper into five or six segments along prominent grout lines (see photo on page 230). Then, remove the cartoon and sticky mesh from the temporary substrate. The easiest way to do this is with the aid of a flipper board—a board that you

Use kindling and logs under 3 in. diameter to keep the fire from burning too hot.

On a crisp evening, gather friends and family around the warmth of a fire.

use to flip the composition over. The board can be any flat, lightweight board you have on hand—a spare piece of wood, plastic, or wedi board. As long as it's slightly larger than the segment you're working on, it will work.

To safely remove your composition, place the flipper board on top of it. Hold both the top and bottom boards (the bottom being the temporary substrate) securely—with the tesserae sandwiched safely in between—and simply flip them over. After you've executed the flip, the temporary substrate will be on top of the pile. Remove it and face it right-side up on your work surface. Apply thin-set mortar to the chimenea, on top of the scratch coat—but only to the area you will set immediately.

8. **Drape-and-set the flame segments onto the substrate.** When a substrate is too heavy to pick up comfortably, you can drape-and-set your composition onto it.

To begin, rotate the segment so that the top edge is closest to you. Using a balled-up cloth, give the composition another sweep over the contact paper. Then, firmly take hold of the corners of the contact paper that are closest to you. Lift the contact paper, and, measuring with your eyes, align the segment with its corresponding position on the substrate, and gently drape the segment onto the substrate. The contact paper holds the tesserae better when you hold it so that it hangs vertically; try to avoid holding it horizontally. Once you've laid it onto the chimenea, you can shift it more precisely into place so that it's positioned exactly where you want it. If any tesserae popped off the contact paper, fit them back into the design. After 30 minutes, gently pull off the contact paper. Repeat this process for the remaining segments of the flame.

9. **Connect the front and back compositions.** Using the direct method, simply continue the flame hair around to the front. This will create a sense of flow and coherence in the mosaic.

10. **Grout, polish, and seal the mosaic as usual.** Follow the directions in Grouting Your Mosaic on page 49.

This colorful lending library will surely be a welcome addition to your neighborhood.

Neighborhood Library

CHALLENGING

I kept the design simple with the word *Library*, but you could personalize your mosaic with the name of the neighborhood or street where it will live.

These little libraries allow communities to share their books. Once you've read a book, you donate it to the library and trust that it will find its next reader. Mosaic is a good way to give the library personality and make it a cherished landmark in your neighborhood.

You can buy a library structure or build your own box, or you can do what I did, which was to recycle an old cabinet that I found at a home reuse center. The one I used for this project is 16 × 20 × 15 in., with a single shelf inside. Of course, the selection of cabinets available at your local reuse center will vary, but for this project, try to find one with similar dimensions. I built a sturdy roof and reinforced the cabinet with panels of cement backer board—and then, of course, added the mosaic!

If you decide to make your own library structure, keep in mind that this project requires some prowess with woodworking. You'll also need to have a window made of acrylic plastic cut to order. If you'd like to buy a structure, Little Free Library (littlefreelibrary.org) is a good resource. Even with a premade structure, you'll have to screw panels of cement backer board onto the surfaces you plan to mosaic.

In the how-to instructions, we'll first go through the steps for designing and building the structure. If you elect to purchase a premade library, you can skip ahead to the mosaic how-to. Don't be shy about

237

Materials

For the cabinet:
- Recycled cabinet
- Plywood (depends on the size of the library; this project needed $4 \times 4 \times 5/8$ in. for the door, roof, and base of the addition)
- Acrylic plastic window for the door, cut to fit
- Four sawtooth hangers
- Four L-braces
- Screws (3/4 in., 1 1/2 in., and 2 1/2 in.)
- Doorknob (optional; new or secondhand)
- 16 ft. of 2×2 in. lumber (for the frame and rafters)
- One 3×5 ft. piece of 1/4-in. cement backer board (avoid using 1/2-in. cement backer board which is too heavy for this application)
- Fiberglass mesh tape
- Roofing paper (about 4 sq. ft.)
- Roof flashing (22 in.)
- Roofing nails
- Roofing shingles, one package
- Primer (optional)
- Paint (optional)

For the post:
- 8 ft. of 4×4 lumber (or 4×6 if your library is especially heavy)
- 8 ft. of 2×6 lumber
- Twelve $3/8 \times 3\,1/2$-in. galvanized lag screws with corresponding washers
- Ratchet set

For the mosaic:
- Stained glass
- Ceramic tile
- Letter tiles (optional)
- Sticky mesh
- Clear contact paper
- Thin-set mortar
- Cementitious grout
- Grout sealant

Tools
- Rock tumbler
- Gloves
- Tape measure
- Jigsaw (or circular saw)
- Drill
- Staple gun
- Construction glue
- Hammer
- Felt-tip marker
- Ceramic tile cutter
- Pistol-grip glass cutter
- Glass runner
- Two-wheeled nipper
- Painter's tape
- Dust mask
- Bucket
- Bowl
- Flat mixing trowel
- Notched metal trowel
- Rubber grout float
- Small painter's trowel
- Cotton cloths
- Small sponge

Templates, pages 291, 292

Letter tiles reading *take wing* and a friendly redbird are just some of the fun details that embellish this piece.

mixing *opera* in the mosaic. In my design, I used three: *opus tessellatum* for the brickwork; *opus sectile* for the light bulb, the tree trunk, and some of the custom-shaped leaves; and *opus palladianum* for the crown of the tree.

The mosaic on the library is likely to be touched, so I recommend using a rock tumbler to soften the edges of the tesserae. Remember the care of your neighborhood library. Have someone lined up to maintain it and keep it clean and tended.

1. **Prepare the cabinet.** If you're using a secondhand cabinet, it will need some initial preparation. Replace the existing door—whether it's wood or glass—with a wood door with an acrylic-plastic window to provide both visibility and sturdiness. Cut the new door out of a piece of ⅝-in. plywood. Attach the acrylic plastic window

continued on page 244

This is the original cabinet, which I found at a home reuse center. I liked the cornice on this one.

The frame for the upper addition is finished. Notice the new door on the old cabinet—it's a simple wood frame with an acrylic plastic panel.

I added plywood to the roof and used cement backer boards for the walls of the upper addition. Notice how I taped the joints of the cement backer board walls with fiberglass mesh tape and coated them with thin-set mortar to strengthen them. What's not visible here is the plywood base of the upper addition, which will eventually be attached by screws to the top of the cabinet. It's easier to work on the two structures when they're not attached.

I used the double-direct method to seat the tesserae on the front of the addition. You can see my bank of tesserae on the paper plate. When you're dry laying a simple pattern like brickwork, cut a bank of rectangles in varying colors.

I used several methods to mosaic the back side of the library. The border tiles are ceramic, seated using the direct method. The tesserae for the brickwork are glass, and I seated them using the double-direct-with-slide method. I used letter tiles for the message, *take wing*.

I set the library on its side to create a flat surface to work on. With a simple repeated pattern like a brick wall, have a bank of tiles ready and apply thin-set mortar using a sandwich bag with a corner snipped off as a makeshift piping bag. The piping bag allows you to work quickly in the direct method.

continued from page 239

to the back of the door with four sawtooth hangers, using one at each corner. Before you attach the new door, install the shelf, if the cabinet needs one, using plywood cut to fit, four L-braces, and ¾-in. screws. Then remove the hinges from the original door and use them to attach the new door to the cabinet. Attach the doorknob to the door, if needed.

2. **Construct a frame for the walls and roof of the upper addition.** First, cut the base for the upper addition out of plywood; it should be the same dimensions as the top of the cabinet. Then construct the frame. The open front and back walls of the frame should each be constructed using four pieces of 2 × 2-in. lumber and 2½-in. screws. Use four pieces of 2 × 2-in. lumber to connect the front and back walls of the frame, using two pieces to create one side (one at the top, one at the bottom) and two pieces to create the other side. Screw the base to the bottom of the frame using 1½-in. screws. Construct the rafters next; they should extend beyond the sides of the cabinet by approximately 4 in. to make eaves that will protect the library from rain. Where the rafters will touch the frame, make a small notch in the rafter to allow the rafter to seat itself on the frame and be secured by the screws. Cut a 30-degree angle into the ends of the rafters that will meet at the peak, and screw them together using 2½-in screws. Last, join the top corners of the two rafters together from front to back with a 2 × 2-in. ridge piece.

3. **Add walls to the frame. Measure and cut the cement backer boards for the walls of the addition.** Using 1½-in. screws, attach the cement backer boards to the frame. Then use fiberglass mesh tape to connect the boards at the corners (be sure to wear gloves when you use fiberglass mesh tape), as you would for sheet-rocking a wall. The fiberglass mesh supplies additional rigidity to the structure and also creates a continuous surface for the thin-set mortar and grout.

4. **Add a roof to the frame. Use two pieces of plywood, cut to size to fit over the rafters.** Screw each piece into the ridge piece and rafters with 1½-in. screws. Attach roofing paper to the surface with a staple gun. Use construction glue to glue a piece of roof flashing over the joint between the roof boards at the top. Nail down the flashing with roofing nails; be sure that the flashing overlaps the roofing paper. Shingle the roof, starting at the bottom and nailing the shingles up to the top of the roof, covering the flashing.

5. **Prime and paint the exposed wood surfaces.** Making large three-dimensional mosaics is time-consuming, so you shouldn't feel as if you have to mosaic the entire surface of the library. Prime and paint the areas that you don't want to mosaic, to protect the exposed wood from the elements.

6. **Secure the cartoons and sticky mesh to temporary substrates.** Lay the cartoons face-up on the temporary substrates and place sticky mesh—sticky side up—on top of the cartoons. If the sticky mesh inhibits your view of the design, use a marker to darken the lines of the cartoons. Then, tape down the corners with painter's tape to affix the cartoons and sticky mesh to the substrates so that your work surface and design will be secure and properly aligned while you lay the tiles.

7. **Dry lay or seat the tesserae.** To seat the tesserae for this project, use whichever method feels most comfortable for you—direct, drape-and-set, or double-direct-with-slide. I used both the direct and double-direct-with-slide methods, depending on what seemed appropriate for the panel. If you'd like to use the drape-and-set technique, follow the directions in the Friendly Raccoon Face mosaic on page 93. And if you'd like to use the double-direct-with-slide method, follow the directions in Double-Direct-with-Slide on page 152. If you'd like to use the direct method, follow the directions in step 4 in the Orb Fountain project.

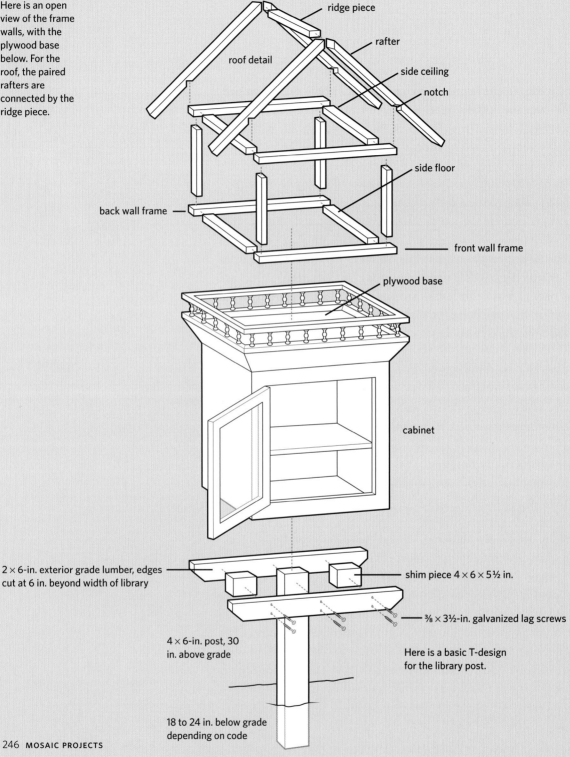

Here is an open view of the frame walls, with the plywood base below. For the roof, the paired rafters are connected by the ridge piece.

ridge piece

rafter

roof detail

side ceiling

notch

side floor

back wall frame

front wall frame

plywood base

cabinet

2 × 6-in. exterior grade lumber, edges cut at 6 in. beyond width of library

shim piece 4 × 6 × 5½ in.

⅜ × 3½-in. galvanized lag screws

4 × 6-in. post, 30 in. above grade

Here is a basic T-design for the library post.

18 to 24 in. below grade depending on code

8. **Grout, polish, and seal the mosaic.** Follow the directions in Grouting Your Mosaic on page 49. Grout just one or two sides at a time so that you don't need to turn the cabinet over as you work.

9. **Attach the upper addition to the cabinet.** Set the upper addition onto the cabinet and use 1½-in screws to screw them together from underneath the top of the cabinet.

10. **Add the post.** For the post, use a 4 × 4 (or 4 × 6 if your library is heavy). Attach two 2 × 6-in. pieces of exterior-grade lumber in a T-design. When you cut the post length, make sure to allow for the section that will be in the ground (18 to 24 inches—check your local code to be sure). Also, don't make the post too tall, since kids will be accessing the library. Aim for approximately 30 inches above ground. Cut the post at 54 in. (or the length appropriate for your library), and then cut two 4 × 6 × 5½-in. shimming pieces. (You'll have to use a circular saw on this cut, but if you have access to a chop saw, that will work even better.) The shims, along with the 4 × 6 post, will become the connections for the 2 × 6-in. pieces. Lay the T design with the shim pieces propping up the 2 × 6-in. pieces. Predrill a hole through the 2 × 6 pieces into the 4 × 6-in. post and use six lag screws per side, with washers. Tighten the lag screws using a ratchet.

11. **Install the library.** Set the post into the ground and screw through the base of the cabinet into the top of the post using eight to ten 1½-in. screws. If you've never installed a post, I recommend asking a contractor for help. If you're installing the neighborhood library in a public place, be sure to get any permissions you need.

Have a little celebration! Invite neighbors for a housewarming party and ask each of them to bring a secondhand book to donate to the library.

This orb fountain brings in the relaxing and nourishing element of water—a must-have for any thriving garden.

Orb Fountain

MODERATE

There's nothing like a fountain to add a relaxing feel to any environment. Water was the natural inspiration for the design of this mosaic. The pattern starts at the top and radiates out and downward symmetrically, mimicking the flow of water from the top. *Opus musivum* gives a sense of the circles radiating out, like water rippling in concentric circles.

Cement orbs, pedestals, and basins can be purchased at garden-supply stores. You can also custom-order an orb with a ⅝-in. channel hollowed out for the water tube to pass through. Choose a water pump that pumps at least 65 gallons per hour, which is enough to give the water the necessary lift. Otherwise, there won't be enough pressure to force the water to the top of the tube. Also, choose a medium-tone grout—a lighter grout will show stains too readily.

1. **Install the pump in the cement orb.** Insert the brass-fitting barb into one end of the vinyl tube. Feed the other end of the tube down the cored-out channel, leaving the barb sticking up ¾ in. above the surface.

Materials

- Cement sphere with ⅝-in. channel, plus pedestal with a channel, and basin
- 2 ft. of ⅜-in. clear vinyl tubing
- ⅜-in. brass fitting barb
- 65-gallon-per-hour water pump
- Three or four bricks
- Stained glass
- Thin-set mortar
- Urethane grout
- River rock (optional)

Tools

- Felt-tip marker
- Pistol-grip glass cutter
- Glass runner
- Two-wheeled nipper
- Sanding block
- Painter's tape
- Dust mask
- Bowl
- Flat mixing trowel
- Sandwich bag
- Notched metal trowel
- Small painter's trowel
- Rubber grout float
- Cotton cloths
- Sponge
- Bucket

Template, page 293

The bright orange petals are a wonderful contrast against the blue.

Secure the tube with thin-set mortar by holding the barb in place as you work. Use a small painter's trowel to fill in the surrounding crevice with thin-set mortar. Make sure the barb is centered. As you work on the rest of the mosaic, check the barb periodically to make sure it stays upright as the thin-set cures.

2. **Assemble the pedestal and base.** The orb will sit on a pedestal base, and the base must sit on bricks in order to let the tube pass through; otherwise the flow of water will be blocked. Place three or four bricks in the basin, place the pedestal on top of the bricks, and place the orb on the pedestal. The pedestal will elevate the orb and create room for the tubing to reach it, and it allows the orb to be more visible.

3. **Draw your design on the surface of the orb.** I opted for a design using radial symmetry (parts arranged equally around a central axis), so I made a stencil of one design and then repeated it five times on the surface, using a protractor to measure the angles (360 degrees divided by 5). Once you've made a stencil of your design, trace around the stencil on the orb where you want to use it. The lower half of the mosaic will not be very visible, so it's not necessary to design anything elaborate for that area.

4. **Hand-set the tesserae using the direct method.** Prepare the thin-set mortar by following the directions in Preparing and Applying Thin-Set Mortar on page 42. Given the round shape of the orb, the direct method is the best way to seat the tesserae. Set the principle elements—the stenciled designs—first, then fill in the background. Working on a small section at a time, use a trowel to spread thin-set mortar on the immediate area. Hand-set each tessera, using both a sandwich bag as a makeshift piping bag (fill it with thin-set and cut off one corner) and a small trowel to both smooth the thin-set and butter the back of the tesserae before pressing them firmly into the thin-set. Let the thin-set mortar cure for 24 hours.

5. **Grout the mosaic with urethane grout.** Urethane grout has a
    built-in adhesive to make it stronger, and it provides a watertight
    seal, so it's the best option for a fountain. It tends to dry fast and
    is harder to clean, so it's best to grout and clean one section of the
    mosaic at a time, in less than 15 minutes each. Grout a small area
    of the orb—approximately 10 × 10 in.— then stop grouting and use
    a damp sponge to clean the grouted area. Scrub repeatedly in a
    circular motion to get the excess grout off the mosaic surface. (You
    need to use more elbow grease when you're working with urethane
    grout.) After you've cleaned the area, proceed with the next section
    of the mosaic.

From a bird's-eye view, you can enjoy the
pleasing symmetry of the radial pattern.
Notice how I used a simple border on the
basin to tie the two pieces together.

6. **Hand-set the pattern on the rim of the basin.** Use a sanding block
    to soften the edges of the tiles for the rim of the basin. For the pat-
    tern on the rim of the basin, I used five orange tiles, set equidistant
    around the rim, and surrounded them with three rows of light blue
    tiles. When you're working with a repeated pattern such as the one
    on the rim of the basin, the direct method is most efficient. Decide
    on your pattern beforehand and follow it through around the rim.
    You can do a quick dry lay of the border to see whether you like the
    pattern before you commit to adhering it. (You don't have to dry
    lay the entire border—just dry lay enough of the border to make
    sure you're pleased with the pattern before you begin adhering the
    tesserae.) Be sure to leave a 1/8-in. space on both sides of the rim
    mosaic to create a shoulder on each side of the design for grouting
    later. When you're sure you're happy with the pattern, remove the
    tesserae, apply thin-set mortar to the rim of the basin (follow the
    directions in Preparing and Applying Thin-Set Mortar on page 42),
    and hand-set the tesserae using the direct method.

7. **Grout the rim mosaic with urethane grout.** Follow the directions
    in step 5 above.

Materials for the orb fountain: a vinyl hose, brass fitting barb, and water pump.

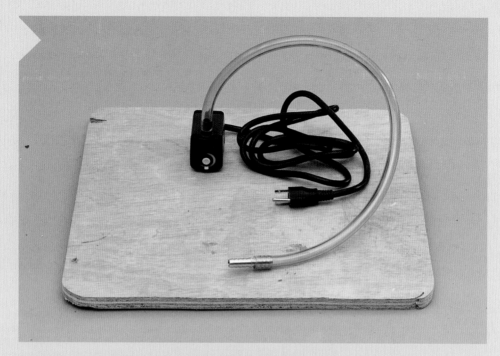

I used stencils to create the main design elements for the orb.

First, I laid the five major design elements.

I used *opus musivum* to expand the circles outward.

This ambitious project is well worth the effort—your senses will delight in the whimsical design and the flowing cascade of water.

Pouring Pitchers

CHALLENGING

This project uses two small ceramic pitchers to create a cascade of water. The design of the mosaic is inspired by water. I envisioned it as a pool or puddle, with water drops pelting the surface, creating ripples. For variety, I made large and small ripples using darker blue tesserae and added some spots of color and pieces of fused glass.

For the best results, I recommend using the exact sizes of the plumbing supplies listed for this project. Once the mosaic is finished, place a small pot in the planter to act as a pedestal for the potted plant—it will keep the plant elevated above the water in the planter.

1. **Prepare the back of the substrate.** To create a space behind the mosaic for the vinyl tubing, use 1½-in. screws to attach two 28-in. pieces of 2 × 4 wood vertically to the back of the substrate, installing the screws through the substrate into the wood and using three screws at the top and three at the bottom of each piece of wood. Using 1½-in. screws, secure the French cleat across the two pieces of wood. Cut a small arch (1½ in. × 2½ in.) in the center at the bottom of the substrate to create an opening for the vinyl tubing and bulkhead to pass through. Determine where you'd like the waterspout to be positioned near the top of the substrate, and drill a ⅜-in. hole for the spout.

The circles are reminiscent of ripples created by raindrops landing on the surface of a pool.

Materials

- 1½-in. screws
- Two 28-in.-long pieces of 2 × 4 lumber
- ½-in. cement backer board, 24 × 36 in. cut with an arched top
- 20-in. French cleat attached (plus the other 20-in. French cleat that pairs with it)
- Two 2 × ⅝-in. L-shaped corner braces
- ¾-in. screws
- 16-in. piece of 1 × 6-in. lumber (for the shelf)
- Four feet of ⅜-in. clear vinyl tubing

Upper fitting:
- ⅜ × ¼-in. brass barb elbow fitting, MIP (male)
- ⅜ × ¼-in. brass barb fitting, FIP (female)
- Hose clamp

Lower fitting:
- ⅜-in. brass bulkhead fitting
- ⅝-in. rubber washer

- 80-gallon-per-hour water pump
- Planter, approximately 6 × 14 × 7 in. (must have flat surface to sit against wall)

- 14-in. length of roof flashing
- ½-in. screws
- Two ceramic pitchers
- Stained glass
- Miscellaneous ceramic pieces (optional; for the flower and random spots)
- Sticky mesh
- Clear contact paper
- Thin-set mortar
- Urethane grout

Tools

- Wet tile saw
- Hammer
- Drill
- Construction adhesive
- Fiberglass mesh tape
- Pencil
- Permanent marker
- Gloves
- Apron
- Safety glasses
- Pistol-grip glass cutter
- Glass runner
- Two-wheeled nipper
- Dust mask
- Painter's tape
- Bowl
- Sandwich bag
- Flat mixing trowel
- Notched metal trowel
- Small painter's trowel
- Rubber grout float

- Cotton cloths
- Sponge
- Bucket

2. **Attach the shelf.** Using the L-shaped brackets and ¾-in. screws, attach the wooden shelf to the front of the substrate, centered between the sides of the substrate and aligned with the bottom edge of the substrate. The shelf will serve as a platform for the planter.

3. **Prepare the fountain.** Measure and cut the length of tubing you'll need to connect the planter at the base to the waterspout at the top of the mosaic. Take into account that the pump will be in the planter on the front of the mosaic and will have a separate piece of tubing as well (you will have enough length of tubing to make both). Then, connect the brass barb elbow fitting MIP to the brass barb fitting FIP. Next, take the other end of the brass barb elbow fitting MIP and insert it into one end of vinyl tubing. Secure the tubing to the fitting with a hose clamp to prevent leaks. This connection will be the top of the hose, or the spigot. Finally, insert the brass bulkhead fitting into the other end of the tubing (this end will pass through the substrate and into the planter in step 5).

4. **Install the spigot.** On the back of the substrate, insert the brass tip of the upper fitting through the hole at the top of the substrate. It should extend about ½ in. beyond the surface of the substrate. The spigot will fit tightly and will be set permanently when the surrounding tesserae are mortared.

5. **Install the bulkhead and attach to the pump.** Feed the bulkhead fitting through the small arched hole in the substrate. Carefully drill a ½-in. hole in the back wall of the planter, near the bottom. Unscrew the brass bulkhead fitting and feed the end attached to vinyl hose through the hole in the planter. Place the rubber washer around the fitting on the inside of the planter, and then screw the brass bulkhead fitting back together. Set the water pump inside the planter and drape the power cord out the top. Attach a short piece

The water flows from the center of the daisy into the first pitcher and pours out the spout into the next pitcher.

of vinyl tubing between the brass bulkhead fitting and the water pump (the tubing should be as short as possible).

6. **Secure the planter.** Cut a piece of metal roof flashing to the length of the planter. Place the metal roof flashing on the floor or a sturdy worktable and, using a hammer, flatten the metal roof flashing. Using construction adhesive and ½-in. screws, secure it to the substrate just above the planter. The roof flashing creates a lip that directs water into the planter. Wearing gloves, take a 2-in.-wide piece of fiberglass mesh tape and tape it across the upper half of the flashing. Apply a layer of thin-set mortar across the fiberglass. This creates a surface for adding mosaic.

7. **Prepare the pitchers.** Cutting and situating the ceramic pitchers is a process of trial and error. (But that's okay. It's all part of the fun!) When you're shopping for old ceramic containers (thrift shops are a good source), choose containers with well-defined spouts—pitchers rather than tea cups, for example. Though the design calls for two ceramic pieces, I recommend picking up some extras in case of error. Expect to cut off approximately 30 to 40 percent of the pitchers on their cross sections. Use a permanent marker to draw a line on each pitcher where you want to cut it. Retain the handle and the lip of the pitcher so that it pours well, and cut the pitchers in such a way that there's a little bit of distance between the spout and the substrate—the cut side of the spout should not rest directly on the substrate. This helps create a waterfall that pours, rather than a waterfall that dribbles down the mosaic.

   Once you've drawn the line on the pitcher, put on your apron and safety glasses, and use the wet tile saw to cut the ceramic. Be sure to cut an even plane so that the pitchers get full contact between the surface of the cut side and the substrate.

8. **Test the placement of the pitchers.** The water should flow from the spigot at the top of the substrate into one pitcher, then into the other, and finally into the planter at the bottom. To test this path, estimate where you think the pitchers should be positioned and adhere them to the substrate with silicone glue; the glue will hold the pitchers temporarily while you test the flow of the water and is easily removed later. Wrap the pitchers to the substrate with plastic wrap for extra hold. This gives you the freedom to test the angle and position of the pitchers and to make adjustments as needed. Pour water into the top pitcher to test how the water flows down. When you find the right spots for the pitchers, mark them on the substrate with a pencil. Then, remove the pitchers and clean off the silicone glue.

9. **Adhere the pitchers to the substrate with thin-set mortar.** To ensure a strong hold, use an extra-thick layer of thin-set mortar. Follow the directions in Preparing and Applying Thin-Set Mortar on page 42.

10. **Create small cartoons for the mosaic and begin to mosaic.** Because of the three-dimensional nature of this mosaic, I suggest completing it in sections and adhering them individually. Then, finish by using the direct method to fill in the final areas. Sketch the circular designs of the mosaic directly on the substrate. Place a piece of vellum paper over one area and trace the design on the paper. These will be your cartoons. Lay each cartoon face-up on a temporary substrate and place sticky mesh—sticky side up—on top of them. If the sticky mesh inhibits your view of the designs, use a marker to darken the lines of the cartoons. Then, tape down the edges with painter's tape to affix the cartoon and sticky mesh to the temporary substrate so that your work surface and design will be secure and properly aligned while you lay the tiles. You'll use the double-direct-with-slide method to seat the circles on the mosaic.

To make room for the plumbing equipment, the back of the substrate is built out with 2 × 4-in. wood. The French cleat is for hanging the finished mosaic.

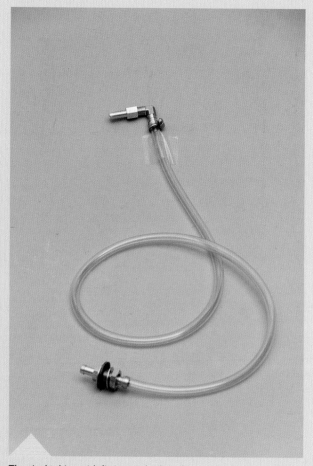

The vinyl tubing with fittings at both ends.

The plumbing installation is complete. The pump will recycle the water that flows into the planter.

Draw a line on the ceramic containers to guide you as you cut them. You should only cut 30 to 40 percent of the piece off, so that there's some distance between the spout (or lip) and the cut edge where the container will attach to the substrate, and be sure to cut an even plane so that the container connects fully to the substrate.

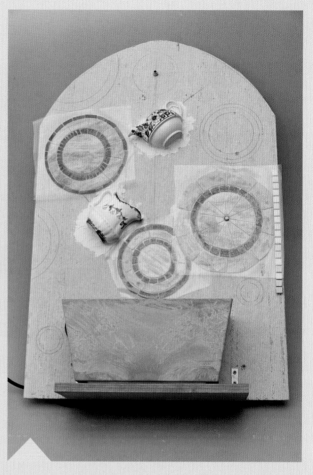

It's time for the big test. Does the pump have enough lift? Are there any leaks? How's the pressure for the water flow? Properly positioning the pitchers takes a bit of patience. Securing the pitchers to the substrate with plastic wrap is a good way to temporarily hold them in place. You may also need to use a little bit of silicone glue where they're attached to the substrate to temporarily keep them from leaking.

The pitchers are attached to the substrate with thin-set mortar, and I've begun to work on the mosaic.

Here you can see the design concept growing. I used ceramic pieces from broken dishes to create a daisy around the fountain spout. Not only is this a pretty design detail, it creates stability for the spout too.

A few touches of color add some variation to the blue. I like to think that the yellow suggests some sunshine breaking through on a rainy day. Fused-glass leaves and the daisy at the top bring in some bright touches of nature. The blue-and-white spiral piece is the bottom of an old bowl.

continued from page 259

11. **Dry lay the tesserae for the circles.** Dry lay the circles directly on the sticky mesh over the cartoons. When you get to the edges, remove the painter's tape so that the tesserae can properly adhere to the sticky mesh. Finalize the design at this stage and check the borders to ensure that no tesserae have crept over the edges of the cartoons. Mark this finished area on the substrate with a pencil so that you know where to apply thin-set mortar later.

12. **Cover the circles with contact paper.** Take a sheet of contact paper, slightly larger than the composition, and gently place it—sticky side down—on the surface of the mosaic, locking all the tesserae in place. Press the contact paper firmly onto each and every tessera, being mindful of the sharp edges under the contact paper. Use a balled-up cloth to press the tesserae down, to avoid cutting yourself.

13. **Lift the circles from the temporary substrate.** Using two corners of the contact paper, lift each circle and place them face-side down on a board, which will later be used to slide the circles onto the substrate. Remove the cartoons and the sticky mesh. Once again lift the circles, this time placing them contact paper–side up (face-side up) on the slider board.

14. **Apply thin-set mortar to the substrate.** Working on one area at a time, apply thin-set mortar to the substrate where you want to place the circles. Follow the directions in Preparing and Applying Thin-set Mortar on page 42.

15. **Slide-and-set the composed circles onto the substrate.** Carefully pick up the slider board and grab a corner of the contact paper. Measuring with your eyes, line up the composed circle with its

corresponding area on the substrate. Slide the mosaic directly onto the substrate by touching down one corner and then slowly pulling the board out from under the composition.

16. **Fill in the background of the mosaic using the direct method.** Once you seat the circles, use the direct method to fill in the background and set the border. Working on a small section at a time, use a trowel to spread thin-set mortar on the immediate area. Hand-set each tessera, using both a sandwich bag as a makeshift piping bag (fill it with thin-set and cut off one corner) and a small trowel to both smooth the thin-set and butter the back of tesserae before pressing them firmly into the thin-set. Let the thin-set mortar cure for 24 hours.

17. **Grout the mosaic with urethane grout.** Urethane grout has a built-in adhesive to make it stronger, and it provides a watertight seal, so it's the best choice for mosaics that will be in constant contact with water. It tends to dry fast and is harder to clean, so it's best to grout and clean one section of the mosaic at a time, in less than 15 minutes each. Grout an area that is approximately 10 × 10 in., then stop grouting and use a damp sponge to clean the grouted area. Scrub repeatedly in a circular motion to get the excess grout off the mosaic surface. (You need to use more elbow grease when you're working with urethane grout.) After you've cleaned the area, proceed with the next section of the mosaic.

18. **Start the fountain.** Fill the planter with water, plug in the pump, and enjoy the fountain!

PROJECT TEMPLATES

Address Sign Numbers

0 1 2 3 4

5 6 7 8 9

Address Sign Vine

Bird Feeder

Friendly Raccoon Face

Spiral Stepping-Stone

Avocado

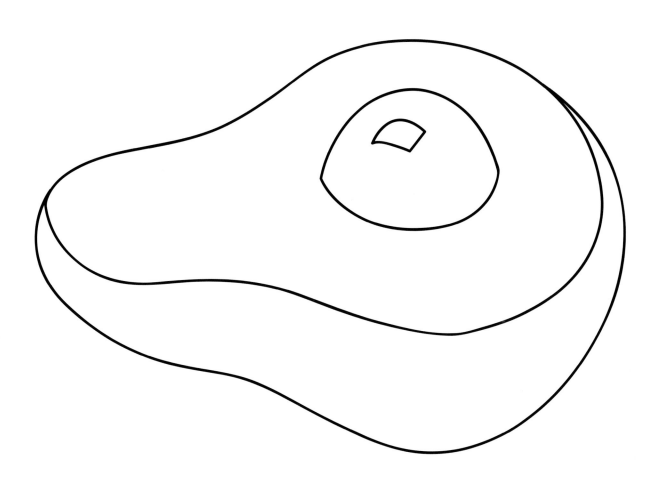

Broccoli

Strawberry

Hosta Leaf

Labyrinth

Bamboo Stand on Recycled Window

Chicken Coop

Flower Tabletop

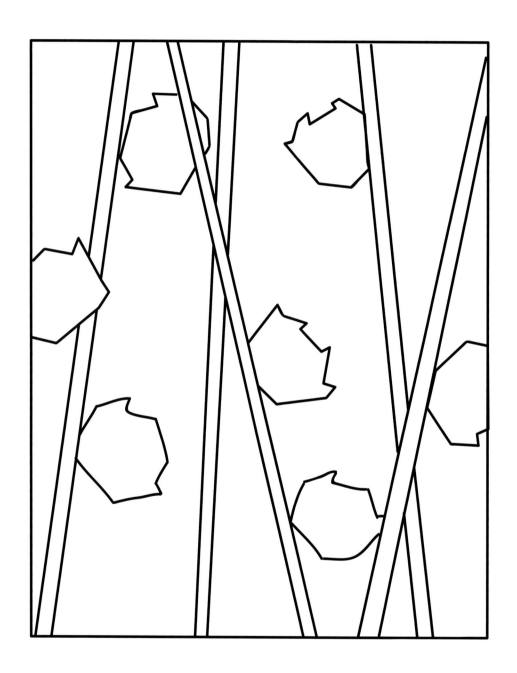

Round Tabletop

Dragonfly

Flowing Wave

Tulip Mosaic with Plant Box (Upper Portion)

Found Objects

Sundial

Pebble Stepping-Stone

Planter with Mosaic Frieze

Chimenea Smoke

Chimenea Flames

Neighborhood Library Front

Neighborhood Library Back

Orb Fountain

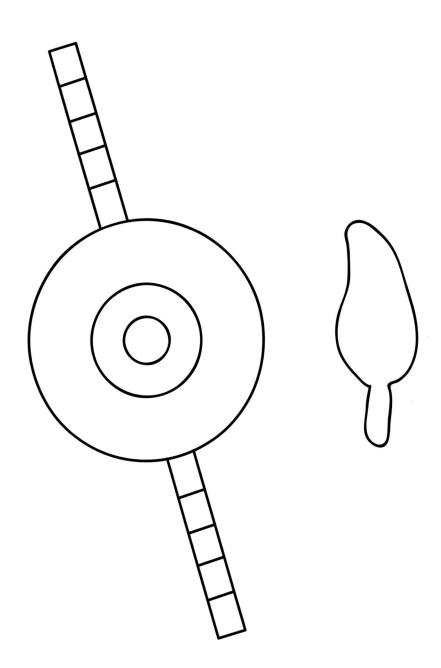

Metric Conversions

inches	centimeters
⅒	0.3
⅙	0.4
¼	0.6
⅓	0.8
½	1.3
¾	1.9
1	2.5
2	5.1
3	7.6
4	10
5	13
6	15
7	18
8	20
9	23
10	25

feet	meters
1	0.3
2	0.6
3	0.9
4	1.2
5	1.5
6	1.8
7	2.1
8	2.4
9	2.7
10	3

Resources

Society of American Mosaic Artists
americanmosaics.org

INTERNATIONAL

Here is a list of suppliers who ship internationally. However, don't forget your local hardware store and warehouse stores like Home Depot and Lowe's for many supplies, including cement backer board, plywood, mosaic-cutting tools, adhesive, grout and grout tools, contact paper, sticky mesh, fiberglass mesh tape, and hangers.

Bullseye Glass
3722 SE 21st Ave.
Portland, OR 97202
bullseyeglass.com
(503) 232-8887
Stained glass and fusible glass

Dick Blick Art Materials
P.O. Box 1267
Galesburg, IL 61402-1267
dickblick.com
(800) 828-4548
Vellum paper, design tools

di Mosaico
3138 East Fort Lowell
Tucson, AZ 85716
dimosaico.com
(866) 437-1985
Italian smalti glass, wedi board, mosaic-cutting tools, medium-strength mesh

Little Baja
1510 E Burnside St.
Portland, OR 97214
little-baja.com
(503) 236-8834
Mexican terra-cotta, garden and patio statuary, birdbaths

Pratt & Larson Tile
1201 SE 3rd Ave.
Portland, OR 97210
prattandlarson.com
(503) 231-9464
A leader in handmade ceramic tile design

Wells Glass Studio
1614 NE Alberta
Portland, OR 97211
wellsglassstudio.com
(503) 719-2728
Fused glass, studio, classes

Wit's End Mosaic
witsendmosaic.com
(888) 494-8736
Mexican smalti tile, vitreous tile,
mosaic-cutting tools

UK

British Association for Modern Mosaics
bamm.org.uk

Mosaic Trader
mosaictraderuk.co.uk

Mosaic Supplies
mosaicsupplies.co.uk

Acknowledgments

Thank you to Sheila Ashdown for patiently putting my ideas and visions into words. Mosaics take awhile, and writing about them takes even longer.

Thank you to my editor Lesley Bruynesteyn, for a skilled hand in finessing the text.

Thank you to my abiding friend Megan Torrance, whose landscape designs make a wonderful backdrop for many of these mosaics. See her work at galahergardens.com.

And finally, thanks to the creative, inspiring, and profound members of the Society of American Mosaic Artists (SAMA). This group of international mosaic artists helps to grow the universal appeal of mosaics. Find out more at americanmosaics.org.

Photo Credits

Photos by Justin Myers appear on pages 1, 2–3, 9, 11, 12–13, 70–71, 72, 75, 82, 88, 90, 96, 98, 104, 110, 116, 124, 132, 136, 138, 146, 147, 154, 157 bottom, 160, 166, 176, 177, 182, 184, 194, 200, 208, 214, 215, 220, 223, 226, 228, 234, 237, 239, 248, 250, 251, 254, 255, 257, 266–267, 304

All other photos are by Mark Brody.

Index

Mark Brody has been teaching mosaic in schools and art centers for over a decade in Portland, Oregon. He has a fine arts degree in sculpture, a certificate in teaching, and is a member of the Society of American Mosaic Artists (SAMA). His website is markbrodyart.com.

As a freelance writer and editor, **Sheila Ashdown** works with authors and publishers to develop well-crafted books that delight and inspire. She holds an MFA in creative writing from American University and is founder and managing editor of *The Ne'er-Do-Well* literary magazine. Find her online at sheilaashdown.com.

Justin Myers is a photographer of characters, from surfers to luthiers, CEOs to ultrarunners, all in their wild natural environments. Along with his wife, he can be found chasing his son, waves, and photographs in and around Oregon.